By the same author

Naval Command and Control
Brasseys 1989

The Future for the Defence Industry (co-author)
Carmichael and Sweet 1990

Articles in the magazine *Naval Forces*
Monch Publishing 1985-89

Command and Control of Submarine Operations

Command and Control of Naval Operations

The NATO Frigate Project

Unpublished pamphlet (family history)
"Twigs and Branches – Selections from a Family Tree"

© William Pakenham 2007
Sometimes at Sea

ISBN   978-0-9555012-0-3

Published by
Talbot Court Press
Croft Mews
Winchester Road
Botley
Southampton
Hampshire
SO32 2BX

email: talbotcourt@pakenham.org.uk
website: www.pakenham.org.uk/talbotcourt

Book designed & produced by:
The Better Book Company Ltd
Forum House
Stirling Road
Chichester
West Sussex
PO19 7DN

Printed in England

SOMETIMES AT SEA

GLAD MEMORIES OF A NAVAL LIFE

Captain William Pakenham
Royal Navy

This book is dedicated to the memory
of those, named and unnamed,
featured in its pages.

The Author ~ Greenwich, 1978.

O Eternal Lord God,
Who alone spreadest out the heavens,
and rulest the raging of the sea;
Who has compassed the waters with bounds
until day and night come to an end:
be pleased to receive
into Thy almighty and most gracious protection
the persons of us Thy servants,
and the Fleet in which we serve ...

(The Naval Prayer)

CONTENTS

LIST OF ILLUSTRATIONS

INTRODUCTION

S*ometimes at Sea* has that special mixture of fascination and pleasure that every good memoir requires. There are a number of interlocking reasons for this. As his subtitle implies, Bill Pakenham's memories are 'glad' ones. No trace here of the bitterness, resentment and self-justification that so often disfigures the genre. Bill greatly enjoyed his life in the Royal Navy and as a result his book is an inspiring rather than a dispiriting read.

The great strength of *Sometimes at Sea* is its blending of the major politico-military events and shifts of the period 1940 to 1979 with the human observations of a kaleidoscope of people and institutions, and those singular communities on board ship. Bill has a keen observer's eye for episode, detail and personality. You can smell and feel the moments captured in these pages, from the ghastly fug of a World War Two troop train to the enervating effect of service in Singapore in the days before air-conditioning.

For a professional historian like myself there are especially choice vignettes of the Royal Family's Tour of South Africa, the Abadan Crisis, the very special naval element of the Anglo-American 'special relationship' and the extraordinary world of the 'War Book' planners during the Cold War. A career that spanned youthful service in HMS *Vanguard*, the last of the Royal Navy's great battleships to, in his professional maturity, refining the nuclear retaliation drills for those new capital ships of the deep, the Polaris submarines, also sheds light on a period of remarkable technological, strategic and doctrinal change.

The ultimate pleasure of the book, however, is the wisdom and humanity that Bill has brought to its pages.

Peter Hennessy FBA
Attlee Professor of Contemporary British History
Queen Mary
University of London

PREFACE

It was the King of Hearts in *Alice in Wonderland* who when asked how a piece should be read replied, "You should begin at the beginning and go on to the end, and then stop." That is not how I have planned this book.

It is in effect a collection of stories (a sailor would call them yarns) not in strict chronological order, but set within the wider periods of my life and linked by loose narrative. It can therefore be read straight though, or dipped into.

I am most grateful to those of my family and friends who have helped in its creation, in particular my daughter Katherine without whose gentle insistence it would not have been started, and who made many invaluable suggestions during its drafting. Also to my wife Antonia, who listened to the drafts as they were written and made many helpful comments.

My research has been confined mainly to my own books and personal records. My memory, such as it is, has been my principal resource.

To those whose understandings of what I have written differ from mine I can only apologise.

Childhood

My first memory is of my third birthday. At breakfast I had been congratulated and presented with a sausage. It was very peppery, and the fiery taste etched my mind. My memories of nursery life are hazy, and I have no vivid impressions of my nannies. I remember Mio my governess, and I was very fond of her. She taught me the 3 Rs, but at this stage of my life I saw relatively little of my mother, and when I was five she went abroad for two years to "pack and follow" my father, who was a successful naval officer and had been appointed to the flagship of the China Fleet. My younger brother Stephen and I, and Mio, lived with our maternal grandparents. Life seemed to be one long round of visits – to our other grandparents, and to various uncles and aunts.

Two years later my mother came back and whisked all three of us off to China for two more years. Long boat trips, and shorter ones – no air travel then. We saw many places – Hong Kong, Weihaiwei, Shanghai, Japan, Singapore, and of course the glamour of the warships. This was when I said that I wanted to join the Navy when I grew up. Together with other naval children of similar age I was tutored by the naval chaplains. At the age of nine I was sent home (with a temporary governess – Mio having left) to go to my prep school, Seafield Park, boarding, where I learned to overcome the pangs of homesickness. I spent the holidays with my grandparents.

I was a year behind in my academic ability, despite the valiant efforts of Mio and my tutors, but I soon caught up and raced up the school, until I reached the second top form where I stuck. The headmaster warned my parents that he could not guarantee me passing the Dartmouth entrance exam. By this time they had returned from China with Stephen, who had joined me at school. They decided that we should change schools, despite the dislocation, and so we both moved to Twyford, near Winchester. It was a first-class school, run by an inspiring headmaster, Bob Wickham, who was much respected in academic circles, and who became one of my role models. I passed the Dartmouth exam, and a little later the daunting Interview (a friendly grilling by an admiral, a captain, and a public school headmaster). In May 1940 I joined Dartmouth. Nazi Germany was over-running France. My childhood was over.

Looking back, it was in many ways what children (particularly boys) of a similar background had to expect in those days. I hardly knew my parents during the first years of my life, which were dominated by nannies and governesses and for some time by my grandmother. I got to know my mother well later, and became very fond of her. I found my father a stern task master, but I knew he had my interests at heart, and I much respected him. He was an important influence on my life, but his long service on the China Station meant that I only saw him for about half my childhood. Later he was at sea for most of the Second World War and I saw very little of him during my formative years. In his absence the task of bringing me up fell to my mother.

What did irk me, I realized later, was the continual moving, from house to house, to lets and hotels and long visits away, with the constant packing and unpacking. By the time I was in my teens I longed for the certainty and stability of a settled home life. I was able to provide this for my own family, later, in spades.

Part One

AFLOAT

… Preserve us from the dangers of the sea,
and from the violence of the enemy;
that we may be a safeguard
unto our Sovereign Lady, Queen Elizabeth,
and her Dominions,
and a security to such as pass on the seas
upon their lawful occasions;
that the inhabitants of our
Islands may in peace and
quietness serve thee our God; …

(The Naval Prayer)

1

Fleet Flagship

On a cold morning in early January 1944, six young mid-shipmen, aged seventeen, joined their first ship at Rosyth. She was HMS *Duke of York*, flagship of Admiral Sir Bruce Fraser, C-in-C Home Fleet. It had been one helluva journey.

The distance from London to Rosyth is about 400 miles, which in wartime troop trains would have taken two days and one night. In fact, we had travelled over 800 miles, by way of the Orkneys and back, which had taken a week. Our joining instructions had not stated where to go, and our travel warrants had specified Scapa Flow, the Fleet base in the Orkneys. Our new ship, the *Duke of York*, had become the nation's darling, having led the force which had sunk the German battleship *Scharnhorst* at the Battle of North Cape some three weeks earlier, thus removing a scourge to the Russian convoys. She was now giving leave.

My mother had taken me to Euston Station, all my uniform etc packed into my new tin trunk. On the platform there was no one to turn me over to, so we kissed and said goodbye. Poor woman, her husband was in the Navy and abroad, her second son at Dartmouth, and here was her oldest off to face "the dangers of the sea and the violence of the enemy". I am afraid I was too excited to fully recognise what her feelings must have been. I found my companions, and we joined the naval troop train. This was officially named HMS *Jellicoe*, and was under the command of a naval officer, a Commissioned Master-at-Arms, one of the naval police force, who had a troupe of tough Regulating Petty Officers (RPOs) to keep order. The naming of the train was to turn it into a "commissioned ship" and give its CO full powers of the Naval Discipline Act over its naval cargo. The fact that the engine driver, fireman and guard actually moved it seemed incidental.

We soon discovered that practically everyone knew that the *Duke of York* was in Rosyth, not Scapa. But there was no overlooking our instructions, and we slowly chugged north. Wartime troop trains moved people, herded eight to a compartment, and did little else. There were indescribable loos, but no sleeping berths, and no restaurant cars. The train stopped three times a day for two hours so everyone could eat at the station canteens. The RPOs guarded the station exits to frustrate would-be deserters, and emptied the station and mustered all onboard before we moved off again. After three days and two nights like this we arrived at Thurso. It was at least good to get out.

We still had to get to Scapa Flow and this meant crossing the Pentland Firth, the stormy strait between Scotland and the Orkneys. We were herded into a commandeered motor fishing vessel, still stinking of fish. You could take your pick, between decks – warm, confined and smelly; or on deck – cold, open and less smelly. I remained on deck. The passage took two hours. Everyone was seasick. By the time we arrived at the base ship, HMS *Dunluce Castle*, a dirty, rat-infested requisitioned merchantman, painted grey and flying the white ensign, there was not much left of us.

Onboard, of course, we knew what to expect. *Duke of York* was in Rosyth. We would have to wait until a ferry returned to Thurso, and then go back. After two days of enforced idleness we did so, via the Firth, just as rough, and the train – just the same. We got out at Rosyth Halt, to find it deserted, but telephoning produced a naval bus. We had arrived.

-----o0o-----

The previous four years, 1940 to 1943, at Dartmouth Naval College may not have prepared us for that journey, but they certainly delivered six well-trained midshipmen to their first ship. I could write a whole book on the most formative period in my life, but a summary will do. Dartmouth was still 'thirteen year old entry', and it gave us an excellent broad public school education, plus a thorough naval training with an officer's indoctrination. Academically it did this by eliminating Latin and Greek, adding Navigation, Seamanship and Engineering, and working us hard. We were streamed into sets from the start, and the top set (the Alphas) was split in the final year and specialised to enhance either Maths and Science, or Modern Languages. I was Alpha Maths, and we were told on leaving that we had reached university entrance standard.

We were taught to sail all types of boat, to row them (known as pulling) and to handle (drive) motor picket boats. There were all manner of games: rugger, soccer, hockey, tennis, squash, athletics, and swimming, and we were taught to shoot, to march and parade, and to handle a rifle at drill. There was much emphasis on OLQ (officer-like-qualities), in particular the importance of initiative. We wore cadets' uniform, and there was a strict code of dress and behaviour (the guff rules), breaches of which – such as a jacket button undone – were punished with the cane (known as cuts), pitilessly applied by one's house cadet captain. On leaving my prep school to go to Dartmouth, Bob Wickham the headmaster had written 'William is still untidy. The Navy will have to correct this.' It did!

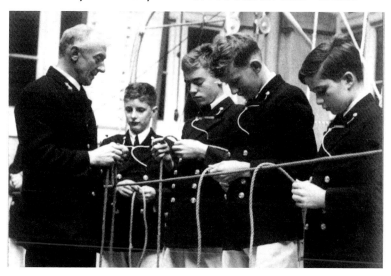

Learning the Ropes. Dartmouth Cadets, 1940.
Author second cadet from left

In 1943, in a sneak fighter-bomber raid the Germans bombed the College. Fortunately we had not returned from summer leave, and there was only one casualty and relatively light damage. After a few weeks the junior terms went to temporary quarters in Bristol, whilst the seniors returned and continued amidst the ruins. I must be one of the very few naval officers who have seen the moon through the missing roof of the galleried assembly hall known as the Quarterdeck!

The College moved for the rest of the war to Eaton Hall near Chester, where I spent my final year. Considering how tailor-made the facilities were at Dartmouth, the authorities reprovided them remarkably well, although the River Dee at that point was a poor substitute for the wide reaches of the Dart. In my last two terms I was promoted Cadet Captain, and then House Cadet Captain. I passed out near the top of my term and collected near maximum seniority as a result.

-----oOo-----

Actually joining our first ship, after that week, was something of an anticlimax. HMS *Duke of York* was alongside in Rosyth Dockyard, giving leave, with few on board, and boiler cleaning. As midshipmen, or "snotties", we were the lowest form of naval life; we were also the only members of the ship's company who had not just taken part in the glorious victory. We settled in to our new existence in the gunroom, the junior officers' mess. For me there was one more rude shock. As midshipmen we slept in hammocks, and had been well prepared at Dartmouth as to how to rig them and sling them. We chose our own billets, spaced pairs of steel hooks on the deck head, and I decided not to join the others in the crowded and stuffy midshipmen's hammock flat, but slung mine outside in the passageway. On getting into my hammock the first night I looked to see how to turn out the light directly over my head, very useful for reading before going to sleep. To my horror I found it was a "police light", and therefore never turned out, indeed no switch. The adaptability of youth came to my rescue, and after one or two

HMS *Duke of York.*

Photograph A30080 courtesy of the Imperial War Museum, London

miserable nights I learnt to sleep in a continuous glare. I have often wondered if my subsequent ability to get to sleep easily was due in some measure to this experience.

A midshipman was still under training, some of it as formal instruction, most of it learning on the job. It was recognised that you would make mistakes but they would not blot your copybook. We certainly had much to learn; perhaps the most dramatic was being "midshipman of the boat". Although you had an experienced senior rating as coxswain, you were in charge, taking the helm and giving engine orders. We soon found that bringing boats, some of them quite large, alongside fragile gangways in rough waves was quite different to what we had learnt in the still waters of Dartmouth. Even more daunting was navigating boats at night in complete darkness – the UK wartime blackout extended to ports and anchorages. I drove a large twin-engined picket boat, with heavy controls, and made my mistakes, but in the end I learnt to handle them well. This stood me in good stead later.

As midshipmen we were useful but not essential onboard. Aside from formal instruction, and the boats – where we were on our own, we were assistants and errand boys, known as doggies; midshipman of the watch on the bridge at sea and on the quarterdeck in harbour – we learned to keep watches at all hours; and we were attached to divisions, the administrative unit onboard. We had to write up, and illustrate with sketches and figures, large Journals – to "encourage observation, the power of expression, and the habit of orderliness". My action station was midshipman of the rear 14" gun turret – very noisy! Most of the time *Duke of York* was spent at her buoy in Scapa Flow, with the occasional trips to sea for exercises like gunnery practice. There were occasional incidents in the Flow, such as scares that midget submarines had got past the harbour defences, but the main memory I have of this period of my life was extreme boredom, quite stultifying. No social life or contact with girls, other than formally arranged dances with

Wrens – nothing more – and no contact with normal civilisation. All this was not easy for a seventeen year old.

Every so often there were interesting visitors, and the more important stayed with the C-in-C who was a great host, and we saw them all. The King spent three days onboard – much ceremonial, and General Montgomery visited just before D Day. Many well-known stage celebrities came up to give shows in the huge corrugated iron Concert Hall. One of these was the young Yehudi Menuhin – who stayed with Bruce Fraser – and who performed with the massed Royal Marine Bands converted to an orchestra. They played some beautiful music, but as a culture-starved lad I also remember how magical it was to hear him tune his violin!

Once every month or so we would go to sea for an operation. These were all mounted to cover Russian convoys to Murmansk, and at the same time to try and sink or cripple the huge battleship *Tirpitz* which was moored in a northern Norwegian fjord, and a serious threat to them. The method was to escort our carriers to the area, just inside the Artic Circle, and bomb her. Although we did see some action, as the U-boats and a few German aircraft tried their best, there was no surface fighting, which was what was intended. On one operation I was on duty on the Admiral's Bridge; a U-boat had succeeded in torpedoing and crippling a small carrier, and a destroyer. They were stopped, and impeding the force's progress. Bruce Fraser made the signal 'Sink *Bickerton*. If *Nabob* cannot steam sink her also' – the most cryptic signal I have ever seen. The crews having been rescued this was done and we proceeded.

The carriers were still the dangerous old "through-deckers" which had to steer at high speed into wind to create enough wind-over-deck for their aircraft to take off and land, with crash barriers if they missed the arrestor hooks on landing. I shall never forget the time the force had to do this for hours while we waited for the returning planes to land, often delayed by accidents on the flight decks which had to be cleared before others could follow. We were steering east, and the Norwegian mountains started to come into view. They got closer and closer, until we could finally just make out the houses on the shore, before lack of sea room forced us to reverse course.

By this time it was summer, and in the Artic Circle we saw the midnight sun, which dipped in the northern sky but did not set. The weather was mostly good, and despite their hidden dangers the gently heaving seas seemed incredibly beautiful. My love of music was developing fast, but there were only scratchy 78 records to be played on a wind-up gramophone – electronic hi fi years ahead. One of these was of Sibelius's beautiful *Berceuse* from *The Tempest*. I never hear this music without recalling it all.

D Day and the Normandy landings took place, but we were not part of that, just a covering force at sea to make sure the German Fleet did not try and interfere. The war was progressing fast, and the time had come for most of the Navy in the Atlantic to transfer to the British Pacific Fleet, including the *Duke of York*. Bruce Fraser was already there as C-in-C. But my group of mids were not to go too – our time in the rank was running out and we had to be kept nearer home to avoid long transport back. We were landed for a spell of leave before setting out for our new ship – in the Mediterranean.

Admiral Fraser and General Montgomery,
HMS Duke of York, 1944

8

2

The Sunny Mediterranean

We arrived in the Bay of Naples some two months later, having had a very welcome spell of leave at home. Our troopship was full of an international mixture of soldiers – the war was beginning to run down and any number of smaller nations had decided it was politic to declare war on Germany and make their contribution. We had joined her in the Clyde after what was by wartime standards an easy ride. The voyage out had been uneventful, the dull skies and heave of the Bay of Biscay turning to smooth seas and fine weather as we passed Gibraltar – just visible to the north. Here we were in glorious weather in late November 1944 in Naples, with Vesuvius clearly visible. See Naples and die – this was why we had joined the Navy!

The administration of the troopship was run by the Army. Very wooden routine, and loud orders by the public address system. We were leaning over the ship's rail and admiring the view when something we recognised appeared. A gleaming green picket boat – and that signified a C-in-C's barge no less, something we well recognised – sped across the smooth waters of the bay, white spray scattering from its bows. To our great surprise it swooped alongside our gangway, and a flag lieutenant in immaculate uniform and gold aiguillettes jumped out and mounted the ladder. A minute or so later the bullhorn roared out 'Midshipman Pakenham report to the Adjutant's Office'. I did so. There was the flag lieutenant. 'Hullo William,' he said, 'I've come to take you out to lunch with the Commander-in-Chief'. He explained. Vice Admiral Hamilton, who was Flag Officer, Malta where my father was Chief of Staff, was at the moment Acting C-in-C Med, taking the place of Admiral Sir John Cunningham who was in London for a conference. He had heard I was in the troopship and invited me and a friend to lunch.

After a whirlwind tidy-up, the barge sped us ashore, where we were then whisked in a shiny black limousine to C-in-C's official residence. Admiral Hamilton was graciousness itself. This was the "Villa Emma" and he had always dreamed of living in it, as it was so named by a forebear of his, no less than Sir William Hamilton, the husband of Lady Hamilton, and it was here in this house that the famous (or infamous?) liaison with Nelson started, when he was in Naples after the Battle of the Nile. And here *he* was, another Hamilton, 'Commander in Chief, Mediterranean'.

In some awe, we were shown round by the flag lieutenant, David Parry-Price. It was a beautiful Italian villa, almost a palace, all arches and porticos and lovely tiled floors, apparently virtually unchanged since Nelson's day. When the British had captured Naples the previous year it had been commandeered. The villa was on top of the cliffs, with a beautiful terrace overlooking the bay, with a private beach below reached by winding steps. After a gorgeous lunch, and still in something of a daze, we were returned to the troopship. My friends were duly impressed, and I noticed that the Army's attitude to midshipmen had changed somewhat!

Our voyage to join our new ship, HMS *Orion*, now became very complicated, but three weeks later we found her in Piraeus, the port of Athens. We discovered a chaotic situation, probably only found in the final stages of war. Greece had been liberated, and was under the nominal control of the right wing government a few miles up the road in the capital. But a communist organisation, known as the ELAS, was attempting to overthrow it, and was mounting a rebellion. Piraeus was in a state of lawlessness, badly damaged, very few police, looting at night. *Orion* was alongside. Two weeks earlier the sub-lieutenant of the gunroom had gone for a "run-ashore" with the midshipmen, and had driven past a sentry and had been shot dead. Everyone was very shocked. The midshipmen already in the ship were due home for courses and left very soon. Our group, now numbering about ten, were therefore the only members of the gunroom. I was Senior Midshipman, and in charge until the new Sub arrived a few weeks later.

The port of Piraeus was full of "relief ships", Swedish merchantmen, painted white to show they were at war with no one, and full of food for the starving population. Because of the heavy ELAS sniping there were no operational tugs, the crews being on strike. Two of us found ourselves in charge of filthy Greek tugs, with our own naval crews. The wheelhouses were protected with sandbags, and the stokers mastered the coal-fired boiler and engines. We assisted ships berthing, and moved store lighters etc. The relief ships had had enough, and decided to leave. We helped them, towing each ship by the bows to the harbour entrance, slipping the tow, and returning for the next one. Slipping the tow was important – if the ship speeded up and started to tow the tug it would turn sideways on and be "girded", and probably towed under and sunk. By this time the British Army had arrived in greater strength, and despite considerable resistance were beginning to restore order. There was little more that *Orion* could do, and we left for Malta. Were we glad!

-----oOo-----

We all found Malta a very welcome change. The island had had a hard war, but that was nearly over and it was rather frenetically rebuilding its social life. My father was Chief of Staff to the local Flag Officer, Vice Admiral Hamilton (now back in post), and I found myself included in many of the parties. We had come for a boiler clean, a "ship's bottom-scrape", and Christmas, but inadvertently stayed longer. Whilst in dry dock the regulations required the magazines to be connected to hoses, in case of fire, and they were plugged into the hydrants ashore. One night some returning sailors thought it would be a lark to turn the hydrants on. This resulted in the only known case of a ship being dangerously flooded in dry dock. We woke up to find it half full of water. It took a long time to dry and repair everything.

At the end of January the ship experienced a remarkable event, which we also regarded as a great honour. After a week or so of rumours, and much cleaning, the Prime Minister, Mr Winston Churchill and his personal entourage came onboard to stay for a few days. The occasion at the time was referred to as the Malta Conference, although this seems not to have survived into the history books. Its purpose was to enable Churchill and Roosevelt and their Staffs to agree their strategy for the end of the war in Germany and its subsequent occupation, and to coordinate the Anglo/US position for the important tripartite Yalta Conference with Stalin, at which the post-war shape of Europe was agreed. The British contingent arrived in different ways. Churchill himself and his personal staff, including his daughter, Sarah Churchill, and his doctor, later Lord Moran, flew out in an RAF transport aircraft, and stayed in *Orion*.

The British Chiefs of Staff flew in a separate aircraft, and stayed with their respective service chiefs in Malta. Their Chairman, later Field Marshall Lord Alanbrooke, stayed with the Governor, General Schreiber, at St Anton Palace. Anthony Eden – still a young man – came out in another cruiser, HMS *Sirius*, which berthed alongside *Orion*, with most of the political and service supporting staff. President Roosevelt, who we never saw – he

Churchill onboard HMS *Orion*

12

was a very sick man by then, with only weeks to live – came in the heavy cruiser USS *Quincy*, with his staff and supporters. (She seemed vast to us, and berthed alongside just up the wharf.) It was a busy few days, with the main meetings being held in the *Quincy*, but most of the British ancillary ones being onboard *Orion* to avoid Churchill having to move. All ceremonial was waived for the occasion, and we got quite used to people like Anthony Eden, the First Sea Lord, and other bigwigs, coming and going.

Winston Churchill had arrived very late, and we now know that he had become seriously ill during the flight out. He came on board and took things very quietly for a day or so. My Journal records that I thought he looked very old. But he perked up, and was delighted to be living in a ship again – he had crossed the Atlantic in a battleship to meet the President earlier in the war – and had elected to put up onboard *Orion* rather than stay with the Governor, which would have been normal. He did us the honour of having his photograph taken with the ship's company on the quarterdeck, and it was believed to be the only occasion that he had done so. He was seated with the Captain and senior officers, with all the others behind. It was traditional for the midshipmen to sit cross-legged in front in such photos, and as senior midshipman I made sure that I was as close to him as possible!

Our stay in Malta came to an end soon after that, and we went to Alexandria to meet up for exercises with our sister ship, HMS *Ajax*, and the rest of our cruiser squadron. The midshipmen's instruction was pursued intensively, as we were to take our midshipmen's exams before leaving. These duly occurred, and I was pleased to find that I had got "firsts" in everything, and was thus still top in seniority. Following that, us midshipmen all had to do our "destroyer time" – three months in a destroyer, with a few weeks of it in a minesweeper. (The Navy was determined that by the time one was a sub-lieutenant one had seen life in as many types of warship as possible.)

Churchill with HMS *Orion's Ship's Company 1945.*
The author is seated in front on the left

We joined our destroyers by a series of lifts in others going in the right direction, but eventually I joined HMS *Lookout*, one of the modern wartime built 'L' Class. I much enjoyed my three months in her. I was a member of the wardroom (the officers' mess – there was only one) with only about six or so ship's officers – plus a few extras like me, and flotilla staff who moved around. It was all very informal and friendly, and I soon realized why so many of the Navy much preferred destroyers and small craft, quite different from the highly regulated life in battleships and cruisers. We spent most of the time as part of the Anglo-French "Flank Force" – a mixture of cruisers and destroyers from both navies providing bombardment support for the slow advance of the allied armies ashore along the rocky French and Italian Riviera coastlines This was a very pleasant duty since it was not very warlike, with everything running down fast, and which entailed much time in French ports. We found we were very welcome, in particular as the Brits were more popular than the Yanks, who were accused of indiscriminate bombing, and the charge that they had "raped their way across Europe" etc. I also spent a memorable three weeks in an Algerine Class minesweeper, clearing up old German minefields off Italy. You can't sweep mines at night, so we enjoyed the delights of Port Offino and Santa Margaretha by the evening, despite the litter of discarded ammunition everywhere, abandoned by the fleeing Germans only months before.

On rejoining *Lookout*, we went to Malta for a short visit for a boiler clean, and while we there VE Day occurred, the end of the war in Europe. I remember thinking how little the average naval officer or rating was affected by it – most of the navy had not been as personally involved as the army and air force. Celebratory parades etc. but a good excuse for a monumental booze-up. In fact my main memory of it all was the night long carousal – all the ships alongside in the naval dockyard giving leave, sailors drunk ashore all over the town, officers drunk onboard in their own (but mostly other's) wardrooms. I should explain that officers had their own alcohol in their messes, but not the sailors. It was a wonder no one was badly hurt, or ships damaged.

Shortly after that it was time for me to go home at the end of my twenty months time as a midshipman, to become a sub-lieutenant, and do six months "Subs Courses" at Portsmouth. I yet again made my way to Naples, which was the main focus for movements into and out of the Mediterranean, and spent a memorable few days in a pleasant Army transit hotel with some of my group ex-*Orion*. The San Carlo Opera House had been commandeered by ENSA (the Services' wartime entertainment arm). Every Italian musician and opera singer was available "for a song" as it was the only place where anything of musical consequence was being performed. I remember seeing Gigli in *Pagliacci* and *Rigoletto*, and other operas too, with tickets available for pocket money. Eventually our whole group of mids were assembled, and yet again we boarded a troopship, for passage home. It was while we were onboard in the Bay of Naples that the news of the General Election came through. Quite stunning – a Labour landslide and Churchill discarded by the electorate despite his wartime leadership. We had not voted, being too young, but we were all shattered. We sensed that the world as we knew it was facing major changes.

-----o0o-----

I arrived home for a long spell of "foreign service" leave, and helped my mother move to our new home near Portsmouth. The next six months were spent on the last period of general training as a young officer on "Technical Courses", mostly in or near Portsmouth. By this time, after twenty months as a midshipman I was automatically promoted to Sub-Lieutenant, with one gold braid stripe on each arm. (They looked and felt enormous at first!). We were accommodated in the many naval schools in the Portsmouth area, and instructed in the details of naval equipment and its use, skills that were required of junior officers. Gunnery, Torpedoes, Navigation, Signals, etc. We also spent a fascinating spell at a Naval Air Station in Cornwall, being indoctrinated into the arts of the Fleet Air Arm, and learning to fly. It was a very pleasant half year, and I was able to spend most weekends at home. I bought a motorbike to get me around, but sold it at the end – I found it desperately cold!

It was during this period that Hiroshima happened, and the end of the Pacific War. We did not perceive at the time the enormous implications heralded by the successful splitting of the atom, which we had been taught at Dartmouth as a scientific challenge. Very difficult to determine what the arrival of nuclear bombs foreshadowed – were they just bigger and better bombs, or did they betoken something more terrible.

With the war ended we all got forms to apply for our Campaign Medals, which recognized the areas and periods in which we had seen war service. I had only served at sea for twenty months, but I had been in the cadets' anti-parachutist platoon – a sort of Lads' Army – at Dartmouth. To my great surprise I found that I qualified for five campaign medals, two rows of ribbons on one's uniform jacket. At first these were insignificant, most officers had more, and many had decorations for bravery or action, but as the years passed they became rarer and rarer. By the time I was Director at the Staff College at the end of my career I was the only officer with them, and I started to feel old!

3

With The Royals to South Africa and back

On a cold and miserable day in early February 1947, HMS *Vanguard* slipped quietly out of Portsmouth harbour on a long voyage. It was 7.0 o'clock in the morning, still dark at that time of year, and there was no ceremonial despite the fact that we were flying the Royal Standard. We were on the way to Cape Town with the Royal Family on board, for the Royal Tour of South Africa. We did not know it, of course, but we were leaving behind a country that was about to experience the worst winter weather in living memory – the Great Freeze Up, which required the Government to declare a state of emergency.

The Royal Family had come onboard the previous evening, and all the officers had been formally presented to them, in order of seniority. Our names were called in turn by the Captain. We each bowed as we had been taught (inclining the head from the neck only) to the King, to the Queen, to Princess Elizabeth and Princess Margaret Rose. This little ceremony was done with a purpose: having been presented, court protocol then allowed that when we met them on deck or wherever, all that was needed was a smart salute.

-----o0o-----

This moment had been months in preparation, and I shall have to go back a year to cover them. The *Vanguard*, last of the British battleships and the largest, had been building at John Brown's shipyard at Clydebank, a suburb of Glasgow, for most of the war, and was in the final stages of "fitting out" when I joined her in February 1946 as Sub-Lieutenant of the Gunroom. I was in time to get my hand on the final design of the gunroom mess – I found there was no bar! It was not an enjoyable few months; Scottish landladies' digs, combined with rationing (still) and the need to go everywhere by bus made it rather dreary, and I was glad when the midshipmen arrived, the ship was commissioned, and we moved down the Clyde to Greenock for our acceptance trials. The ship was in fact already obsolete – the Pacific War had changed naval concepts for good. The aircraft carrier had replaced the battleship as the capital ship, and the advent of radar and the associated operation rooms had revolutionised the way in which naval warfare was controlled. But as a new ship she had to be "accepted" and paid for, and that meant trials to prove she met her design criteria, and to calibrate her performance and weapons. It was a busy time.

The ship's speed trials were early on, in order to get calibrations of speed against propeller revolutions when she was still "bottom clean" – ie no barnacles. They were conducted off the "Arran Mile", marked by large white transit posts ashore, exactly a mile apart. The most exciting was the top speed trial. Her design top speed was 31 knots – but no one knew what it would be in practice. I was on the bridge as we rang down "Full Speed Ahead", well short of the "Mile", and the ship was going

HMS *Vanguard on speed trials, 1946*

flat out as we passed the first transit posts and stopwatches were started. If it took two minutes exactly to reach the other posts that would mean only 30 knots, and we were on tenterhooks as we approached. We got there several seconds earlier then the two minutes, and top speed was logged as over 31 knots, an excellent result.

The "heavy weather" trials were designed to judge her behaviour in a storm – but we couldn't find a storm in high summer! The most dramatic were the "gun blast trials" – designed to see how close to the superstructure her 15" guns could be trained and fired without causing damage. As this would limit the ship's permitted arcs of fire it was important not to be too lenient, and the determined "trials officer" who conducted them (Mike Le Fanu, later a notable First Sea Lord) was having no nonsense. You didn't know if damage *would* be caused until you caused it. He calibrated the after turrets first, training them lower in elevation and closer astern until he got the results he was looking for. He finally blew the H/F D/F hut (right at the stern) overboard, and scorched the teak decking of the quarterdeck. Next he turned his attention to the forward turrets. 'A' turret, the foremost, caused little problems, some badly scorched paint, but 'B' Turret was just under the bridge. I was again on watch when the guns were trained so close that the blast shattered half the bridge windows (we had taken shelter!). These were made of very special bulletproof glass, 16-ply laminate, and almost unobtainable during the war. John Brown's representative, who had been in charge of the ship's construction, could contain himself no longer. He stormed up to the Captain and shouted in broad Glaswegian 'If this is shipbuilding I'll eat ma hat!' He took his hat off and stamped on it. The Captain judged that the gun blast trials had discovered enough.

-----oOo-----

We were in the final stages of trials when the astounding news arrived that HMS *Vanguard* was going to take the Royal

Family to Cape Town for the Royal Tour of South Africa. This task would normally have been undertaken by the Royal Yacht, but the old *Victoria and Albert* was judged no longer sufficiently seaworthy. In fact it was not the first time that a major warship had been used for such a duty. The pre-war battle cruisers HMS *Renown* and HMS *Repulse* had been converted to support a number of Royal Tours by the Prince of Wales (later King Edward VIII) and by his brother, then the Duke of York. Anyhow, we all felt very honoured by the prospect.

By September we were alongside in Portsmouth for several months of dockyard work to provide the necessary Royal accommodation, and smarten up the ship. The work needed was to alter the layout of the second deck in the after superstructure, to provide the Royal Apartments, and to spruce up the ship generally. We found the dockyard *very* cooperative. This was long before the strict accounting methods of later years, and we found that all we had to say when demanding things – like extra paint, teak gratings, and other goodies to enhance the ship's appearance – was that it was "for *Vanguard*".

There were many other things to be done too. The ship was to remain in South Africa during the two months or so of the Royal Tour, and her programme during this period had to be planned carefully. We would be guests of the ports we visited, and the local dignitaries had to make their own plans for what would be big events. This was all handled by the Captain, who was also in touch with the Palace on the details of the onboard programme during the long voyages out and back. Then there were the changes to personnel – we had to be able to parade a full sized Royal Guard, and a full-sized Band, which meant more Royal Marines. There were one or two obvious "misfits" amongst the officers – "scruffy", or hard drinkers – who found they were urgently required for duty elsewhere, and these were carefully replaced. A further measure was necessary. At this particular time the Navy was very short of men, as "war service only" enlisted personnel had to be de-mobbed. *Vanguard's* complement was nearly 2,000, a big slice of the Navy, and the solution was to offer those onboard who were due for release the option of remaining until the ship returned from South Africa, with the lure of the good time we expected to have. They were known as SAVOLS (South Africa Volunteers), and this scheme nearly backfired later in an unforeseen way. Finally everything was ready on time, and the Captain – W.G. (Bill) Agnew – was promoted to Rear Admiral, as is normal for officers commanding Royal Yachts or the equivalent.

-----oOo-----

We nosed down channel in early February 1947. The voyage ahead was seventeen days long, and the first few of these were not very pleasant, dirty Atlantic weather, not rough but uncomfortable as we made our way at about 18 knots – sufficient to allow for unforeseen delays. It was understood that the Royal ladies were "not feeling too good" and preferred to remain in their quarters. There were, of course, several members of the Royal Household onboard too, the King's Private Secretary, Sir Alan Lascelles, an older man but a very influential one. Then there were two Royal Equerries, one Navy, and one RAF, and the Queen's Lady in Waiting. Not to be forgotten were the essential attendants; assistant secretaries, a valet and personal maids, hairdressers and so on; plus a cross section of the Press – a well known BBC correspondent; an accredited journalist; and a cameraman – who covered the events onboard as well as accompanying the Royal Party in South Africa. The King, who had been a serving naval officer in his younger days much enjoyed life onboard, and often came down to the Wardroom for a drink at the bar before dinner. Warning of this was passed quietly to the Commander, who arranged for a suitable group of ship's officers to be there too. We understood that the whole of the Royal Family thoroughly enjoyed the seclusion of being at sea with no over-attentive press, and a relaxing rest after a demanding war.

The Royal Family onboard HMS *Vanguard, 1947*

Part of the set-up onboard was that we had installed for the trip a very powerful radio transmitter, which enabled the ship to speak by radio telephone to London throughout – unheard of then, decades before satellites. This came into its own within a few days of leaving Portsmouth. The weather in the UK had begun to turn not only very unpleasant, but dangerous. The Great Freeze Up not only dumped snow everywhere with bitter temperatures, but disrupted coal deliveries and transport, and led to power cuts. The Government declared a state of emergency. Although not aware of it at the time, we afterwards understood that the King talked at length to the Prime Minister, Mr Attlee, and considered returning, but it was decided to continue.

The weather improved, as usual, on reaching the latitude of Lisbon, and became balmy as we passed the Canary Islands. By this time the Royal ladies were feeling much better, and the whole family regularly strolled on the starboard side of the large quarterdeck, which was reserved for them. In the evenings the Princesses played 'tag' and other strenuous (but decorous) games with the midshipmen, which led to those famous photographs and newsreels, as the royal cameraman caught them on film. In fact the Princesses were entertained more than once in the Gunroom, where they were able to meet officers of their own age. I was no longer part of this, as my time in the rank of sub-lieutenant had ended; I had reached the seniority which meant I was automatically promoted to lieutenant, and about a month before we left I became a member of the Wardroom.

The main event of the voyage out was the time honoured nautical ceremony of "Crossing the Line", the indoctrination, by means of various awful rites, of those onboard who had not already crossed the equator. The elaborate pantomime concocted by *Vanguard* clearly had the Royal audience in mind. Our first evening in the Tropics – remembering that at those latitudes sunset and sunrise are never very far from 6 o'clock – the ship slowed down and quietly dropped a seaboat carrying a motley crew. It sped ahead of us, and a little while later the ship was instructed to stop by "His Majesty King Neptune" – the order being amplified by loud hailer. The boat came under our bows and its passengers swarmed onboard (via conveniently provided rope ladders). The fo'c'sle was floodlit, and we could see it all, with the ship's company clinging to the guns and superstructure, and the Royal Family on the specially constructed viewing platform just beneath the bridge. There was King Neptune himself, with flowing beard and silver crown, shimmering sea green robes, and of course his gold trident. He was accompanied by a small troupe of Royal Barbers with huge cut-throat razors (made of wood), the famous Sea Bears, and fishlike attendants, all in lurid costume. Neptune spoke in ringing tones via his loud hailer. He was pleased to welcome to his Kingdom His Majesty King George and his Queen, who were deemed to be indoctrinated already, but there were others onboard, including the two Princesses, who had not been, and also a few miscreants who would require special treatment. The Ceremony would be performed the next day. Meanwhile, he was glad to provide a special fireworks display.

The fireworks had all been carefully placed on a large table erected right in the bows, and there were attendants to light them, dressed like ship's cooks. The display had been carefully planned to last about fifteen minutes, and included rockets, Catherine wheels, Roman candles etc. but what happened next exceeded even Neptune's special intentions. Two large Roman candles were lit, and looked magnificent. It soon became obvious that the fireworks were beginning to light themselves from those next door, and the display got larger and larger. Just in time the ship's cooks, Neptune, and his Sea Bears, Barbers and all made a dash for safety – there was a spectacular final explosion, and the display was over. It had lasted a splendid two minutes. The ship resumed its voyage.

Next morning at about midday the Ceremony was performed. A large wooden platform had been put up, with two barber's chairs with their backs onto a temporary canvas swimming bath. They were hinged at the rear, so after "treatment" the sitters could be back-somersaulted into the water, for further "treatment". The Royal Barbers, looking rather like clowns with white top hats, and huge mugs of frothy white lather and shaving brushes, plus their fearsome razors, were ready. The two Princesses were first, and I am sure they had been assured beforehand that their "treatment" would be mild. They were seated in the chairs, and given a dab of lather on their noses, and then presented with a special coloured certificate, signed by Neptune, granting them by Royal Condescension the Freedom of His Seas and exemption from further Homage. Everyone on board got a copy, and mine still hangs in the bathroom. There followed the "treatment" of the miscreants, carefully selected so as to be of interest, but not so senior as to suborn authority. These were smothered in lather and "shaved" by the Barbers, then pitched backwards for a through ducking by the Sea Bears. They all survived with surprisingly good grace!

A few days later in the evening the ship slowed down. We were within a hundred miles or so of Cape Town and the margin of error provided by our speed of 18 knots was no longer required. Next morning, exactly as planned, we steamed past the breakwater into the calm waters of the Port.

-----oOo-----

Vanguard made a perfect alongside, politely declining the help of the waiting tugs, which caused much wonder from the thousands of spectators, some on the top of Table Mountain. The Royal Family were on their viewing platform waving to the crowds, and then moved down to the quarterdeck. After impressive ceremonial, onboard and ashore, they got into the Royal Train which was waiting on the jetty. An hour or so after we entered port they were away – the Royal Tour had begun.

We then enjoyed a fortnight or so of fantastic hospitality, provided by the good and generous citizens of Cape Town and its environs, and expertly organised by the South African Navy, who got the whole thing into a massive printed programme. All of us, officers and men, were welcomed into people's homes, and I could tell one or two stories about it, but will refrain! As far as I was concerned, a twenty year old with a wartime upbringing behind me, it was my first experience of this sort of thing. I remember two things which stood out, apart from the kindness and generosity. The lovely countryside and vineyards of Groot Constantia and Parel Valley, remembering that it was South African summer. The other memory, sadly, was the realisation of how insecure the whites felt the only people we met, of course – relying as they did on apartheid to maintain their position, and basically frightened of the blacks especially at night. It was decades before South Africa changed completely, and much happened on the way, but the cracks were there already. I was not alone in my thoughts – we all felt the same.

-----oOo-----

After two weeks or so of this carousing the ship 'took itself off' to Saldanha Bay, a large and virtually uninhabited estuary about seventy miles from Cape Town on the west coast. With its expanse of water and flat surroundings it was like a "hot Scapa Flow". We exercised, rowed our boats, had picnics ashore (by ourselves) and generally used up the time. Why we went there was not entirely clear. The Captain, who had agreed the ship's programme, had said that after two weeks of Cape Town we would all need a rest. He probably did; he had had a "hard war" as a very successful cruiser captain, and had taken the brunt of the official entertaining in Cape Town. But not many of the officers were in the same category, and the men (particularly the SAVOLS) certainly weren't. But it is possible that there had been other factors. The ship had to wait in South Africa for about two months to take the Royal Family back, and it would have been virtually impossible to devise a programme based on eight weeks continuous hospitality – there were only a few ports large enough to take the ship. Whatever the reasons rumbles of discontent started on the lower deck, particularly amongst some of the SAVOLs who considered they were being short-changed.

This all stopped as soon as we moved off. We spent a few days exercising with the South African Navy, centred on their base at Simonstown. The plan was for the ship then to go up the east coast, and a day later we arrived off Port Elizabeth for a four day visit. The place was a medium sized commercial port, not nearly large enough to allow the ship to enter. The ship would anchor offshore and give leave by means of shore tenders, which would fetch and return liberty men. It all went wrong when we found there was such a heavy swell that these large craft could not berth alongside safely. 'No shore leave today,' was announced. But it did not prevent several tugs with passengers steaming out to see us, with pretty girls waving invitingly, their skirts fluttering in the breeze. We had not given shore leave for nearly a month, and it became obvious that something *had* to be done. An officer was sent ashore by sea boat, and arranged for the tenders to be fitted overnight with hastily constructed wooden platforms at a similar height to our upper deck. We removed guardrails over a twenty foot length, and had sturdy sliding gangways made with handling ropes at either end. The next day the shore tenders were able, very slowly, to take on liberty men for shore leave – and later return. We had to restrict numbers so that if those ashore could not be returned there would still be enough men onboard to steam the ship.

Two very embarrassed officers were sent off to apologise and explain to the local authorities up the coast that HMS *Vanguard's* visit to East London was cancelled; and that the ship would be arriving in Durban three days earlier than on the official programme. Next morning the ship weighed anchor and proceeded to Durban, where we went alongside. We gave shore leave, and three days later picked up the Official Programme. It was Cape Town repeated. No more complaints!

Our final fortnight in Cape Town was more of the same – the way they kept it up was remarkable. There is not much more that I can say; it was wonderful. There was one thing, however, which was different. The day before we left for home I was put in personal charge of about twenty million pounds worth of gold bullion. It had been in South Africa for the war, and the Bank of England had cannily arranged for the ship to bring it back (no transportation charges; no insurance). It was to be stowed for the voyage in one of our magazines, which happened to be mine as Officer in Charge of its gun turret. The magazine was empty, having been de-ammunitioned in Portsmouth. Amidst much evident security – large black vans; large police escorts; wailing sirens etc. – the stuff was brought on board, over 100 heavy wooden boxes, each enclosing a standard gold bullion bar worth about £200,000. They were loaded by sweating sailors onboard into the magazine hoist, and thus below. The regulations required bullion to be in the personal charge of one person only, and I stood in the magazine and counted the cases as they were stowed on the deck in a long pile about two feet high. I then signed a receipt for the cases (no statement of value), which was given to the South African official. The magazine key became mine alone.

This is probably the best place to describe the reverse arrangements in Portsmouth. Soon after we got back a large unmarked black van drew up alongside the ship. No police, no sirens. A little man in a bowler hat came on board and said he had come for the bullion. The reverse procedure was carried out, and the sweating sailors piled the boxes into the van. The official counted them, and gave me a receipt. He locked the van doors, got in, and told the driver to drive off to London. I returned the magazine key to the keyboard.

The day after the bullion arrived onboard the Royal Family returned to Cape Town. It had been a most successful Tour, they had been rapturously received everywhere, and they were now about to make their departure. In the afternoon they came down to the long jetty for the farewell ceremonies. Huge crowds, music, songs – lovely South African ones (I can't remember their names), Scottish ones (*Will ye ne'er come back again?*) – guards, bands, much ceremony, all very gripping. *Vanguard* paraded the Royal Guard and Band, and received the Royals onboard. Then it was all over. We slipped our moorings, the Royal Family waved, and we moved out to sea. The Royal Tour of South Africa was over. However, there was still much to tell about the return voyage.

The Boats Officer became sick, and as his assistant I found myself in his job. Amongst other things this involved driving the Royal Barge, a ship's picket boat (fortunately exactly the same type that I had so laboriously learnt to handle well in Scapa Flow as a midshipman), beautifully decked out in royal blue enamel, with white cotton furnishings etc. This had not been used so far, but was going to be put to good use to land the Royal Family at the island of St Helena, famous as Napoleon's final place of captivity, on the way home. It was the first time a British Monarch had ever visited the place, and there was a special issue of postage stamps. We arrived there after four days at sea and anchored offshore, lowered the starboard gangway and dropped the Barge.

The Royal Family embarked, all dressed in their best. We sped shoreward, but in the little bay which served as a harbour I found to my horror that the islanders had sent out a large and beautifully painted *punt* to take them ashore. We had expected to use the little jetty, but were told by the punt's crew that there was not enough depth of water (one more instance of poor planning). The problem was, the Royal Barge's deck was four feet above the water line, whereas the punt lay flat on the sea. There was no way that the Royal ladies could step down that height, nor could they be carried down. The King decided what to do, everyone to get onto the starboard side to heel the barge and reduce freeboard. That was splendid, but it submerged the boat's exhaust pipe, which spluttered filthy black suds. I at last got the stoker petty officer to understand he was to cut the engine (in the noise he couldn't understand why), and finally the Royal Family got ashore. On return to the ship I explained what had happened, and our shipwrights rapidly made a set of portable steps to put in the punt. A few hours later the return trip went well.

The other occasion I acted in a similar capacity was when the Royals visited the ships escorting us at sea. For much of the homeward leg *Vanguard* had a ceremonial escort of a small aircraft carrier and some destroyers. The King decided it would be correct if he and his ladies could make them a visit, and inspect a parade on the carrier's flight deck – representative personnel from the destroyers being transferred for the occasion. It was obvious that we could not use the Royal Barge as such, since dropping and recovering it from its crane in the swell could have been very difficult if not dangerous. The only suitable craft for such a venture would be a sea boat – that is a motorised whaler with an open deck and no cabin – which could be dropped from its special davits for use at sea. We had one beautifully painted for just such an occasion. Unfortunately the King became temporarily indisposed and the trip over had to be just the Queen and the two Princesses. *Vanguard* stopped so that the ship made a lee on its starboard side, and the main gangway was lowered. There was no difficulty in taking the Royal ladies and the Naval Equerry onboard and over the short distance to the carrier, which was similarly positioned. However, she was a much smaller ship, and the lee at her gangway was not good. The sea boat rose and fell several feet at times, and we had to wait before there was a sufficiently calm patch to allow our passengers to step safely onto the platform at the bottom of the ladder. The attempt was nearly abandoned, but the Queen was determined, and asked me to give her my hand to steady herself. We had to wait standing up until the swell allowed the boat to be safely at rest at the gangway, and I afterwards thought I must have held her gloved hand longer than anyone else on that Tour! But they made it, and fortunately the swell had gone down by the time they returned.

The Royal Family were very hospitable, and often invited officers who had attended on them during the day to have dinner that evening, so twice I found myself at the table with them in the Royal Quarters. On one of these occasions they had a small dance band, provided by the Royal Marines. After dinner we were standing and waiting when the band struck up. I was talking to the Queen, and I suddenly realized that unless she took the floor no else could. Plucking up my courage I asked her very politely if she would like to dance – she was obviously waiting for it and immediately accepted. At the end of that number, Princess Elizabeth came up and said, 'Let's have a conga! – Come on band! – Come on! (to me) – Come on Margaret!' I duly put my hands on her hips, and Princess Margaret put her hands on my hips, and we started to dance with the whole party snaking behind us. The Royal Apartments were interconnected, and at one stage I thought, 'Never again will you dance through the Queen's bathroom, holding the Heir Apparent's hips, with her sister holding yours!'

The final remarkable episode on that remarkable voyage home was when, towards the end, the Royal Family were guests of the Wardroom Mess for our "Saturday Night at Sea" Mess Dinner. This was a fairly rare event, as Saturday was not often spent at sea. When it was, and the mess dined formally, rather than the usual running supper, it was a long standing naval custom for the second toast – the first always being the Loyal Toast – to be 'To Sweethearts and Wives', (and once it had been drunk everyone intoned quietly, 'and may they never meet'). For me it was very special. I was the youngest member of the mess, and it was the custom for that officer to reply on behalf of the ladies who had had just been the subject of the Toast. I can well remember deciding what I was going to say whilst I was having my bath before getting into my mess dress. The secret was to keep it short.

The Royal Family were in great form. For the meal the King sat on the President's right, and the Queen on his left. As speaker I sat at one of end of the top table, with Princess Elizabeth on my left. We drank the Loyal Toast seated – this being a much valued custom granted by Royal permission many reigns ago. We then drank the toast to Sweethearts and Wives, and the President called me to my feet to reply. I started with the formal opening – 'Your Majesties, Your Royal Highnesses, Mr President, Gentlemen.' I started by saying how honoured I felt to represent the beautiful ladies on whose behalf I was speaking. I continued by saying that I thought we would all agree that South Africa had come up to expectations. (Cries of 'Speak for yourself, Bill' – 'What were you expecting?') I ended by saying how much my ladies appreciated the Toast, and that on behalf of those astern of us I would say, 'Thank you for coming', and on behalf of those ahead, 'Thank you for coming back.' It was well received.

Shortly after that the meal ended for "after dinner games". These would normally have been rather boisterous, but were suitably scaled down. We had a sing-song, – one of the officers was an excellent pianist – and then to everyone's amazement the Princesses offered to sing to us! Princess Elizabeth played the piano, and they sang duets – light and humorous songs. We then played one or two fairly sedate games, including the one in which the Mess marches around and sings 'We are the King's Navee, and we want to sail the sea' which the King much enjoyed. There was no doubt about it, that night the Royals "let their hair down". After it was all over I was standing at the bar talking to the Commander when the three newsmen came up. One of them, a cynical journalist, Louis Woolfe, said, 'You might be interested to know that three hardened court correspondents have just seen things that in their wildest dreams they never thought could happen.'

----oOo ----

A few days later we steamed into the Solent on a bright morning in early May. Spithead was crowded with boats and yachts of all sizes and descriptions, intent on escorting HMS *Vanguard* into Portsmouth Harbour. The deep water channel through the mud flats is narrow and winding, and the Harbour Master's launches and police craft had their hands full to stop them getting under our bows. But we made it on time, and berthed safely. There were tremendous crowds there too. Once alongside, *Vanguard* "manned ship" – with the Ship's Company clustered all over the superstructure – and cheered the Royal Family ashore. After due ceremonial, they got into their limousines and drove off with a huge police escort. It was all over.

There were one or two aftermaths. Three days before our arrival I had telephoned my parents (that useful radio transmitter) and asked them to organise a private dance at our new home near Portsmouth for all the young unmarried

The Royal Family leaving HMS *Vanguard*
at Portsmouth, 1947

Wardroom officers, and invite partners for them. Hampshire was scoured for young ladies; there were no refusals.We also invited the Queen's Lady in Waiting and the Naval Equerry. Two evenings later it was a party to be remembered.

The other aftermath happened twenty-five years later. In 1972 several senior ex-Vanguard officers got together and started to organise a "Vanguard Reunion", to include wives, and surviving members of the Royal Household. Careful approaches were made to the Palace, and to everyone's delight the Queen, who had been on the throne twenty years by then, accepted, together with her mother and her sister. The party was at one of the big London service clubs, and Antonia and I flew home from Gibraltar for it. Others flew in from as far as Australia. It was a private royal occasion, and great pains were taken to keep the press away. A special thing about the Reunion was that the Queen asked her mother to take precedence, to mark the fact that she had been Queen for the Tour. These splendid occasions were held every five years with the same guest list until the 50th anniversary in 1997.

HMS *Vanguard* remained in commission as Home Fleet flagship for a few years. A second Royal Tour, to Australia, was planned but the King's illness and eventual death prevented it. Her place was taken by the new Royal Yacht *Britannia*, and in the mid-1950s *Vanguard* was paid off and joined the Reserve Fleet in Fareham Creek. In 1960, and seemingly reluctant, she left Portsmouth under tow for the breaker's yard, but ran aground in the narrow harbour entrance – to the astonishment of the crowds waving her goodbye. After half an hour's heavy effort by numerous tugs she was refloated and resumed her final voyage. The last of the dreadnoughts had had a short but eventful life.

4

Destroyer Squadron

In May 1950 I joined HMS *Saintes* in Malta, having just completed my Long Communications Course, and thus qualified as a signals specialist. I knew Malta well of course, its heat, its smells, and its *bells* – the island is full of churches, and their bells are sounded for every possible reason. *Saintes* was the Leader of the 3rd Destroyer Squadron, and this was a very typical first job for a signal specialist. Her commanding officer was Captain Peter Dawnay, a full "four striper" and his position was known as Captain (D, and although not named as such he acted as Commodore of the Squadron. The captains of the three other ships of the squadron were of lower rank, commanders or lieutenant commanders, and most of the time the four ships acted together as a unit. They were all Battle Class destroyers, the latest in design, but although the leader was indistinguishable from the rest (other than the broad black band on her funnel) very little was done to provide additional accommodation onboard for the specialist Squadron Staff. As a result we were very crowded.

HMS *Saintes, 1951*

This was not my first appointment to a Battle Class destroyer. On return from South Africa in 1947 I had been brought down to earth by being re-appointed for a short commission in a destroyer, HMS *Barrosa*. By this time I had been accepted for specialisation in Signals, and was really only marking time for my Long Course. The next year or so was very unremarkable if only because together with most of the Home Fleet we spent most of it in "suspended operation" (with a greatly reduced ship's company) alongside in Portsmouth. The rapid run-down of naval wartime personnel, unmatched by ships being paid off, meant that the RN could only fully man a squadron of one cruiser and four destroyers, which did not include us. We just kept the ship ticking over. As a result, with my shipmates, I saw much of the clubs and pubs of Portsmouth and Southsea in the evenings, with not much else to report. When the Navy finally got itself organised, the Home Fleet celebrated by going on a splendid cruise to the West Indies, exercising like mad on the way over, and then splitting up into small groups, so that the Fleet visited all the islands. We visited Trinidad, Tobago, St Vincent and St Lucia. The ship got home in time for Christmas, and before she left for the spring cruise I departed to join HMS *Mercury*, the Naval Signal School near Petersfield, a few weeks later in early 1949.

I must admit that I did not enjoy my time in *Saintes* as much as the other appointments in my career, at least not at first. It was mostly my fault – I was inexperienced in the arts of naval signals, and although well trained, there is a wealth of difference between learning it all in a classroom and taking the rapid decisions needed in the hectic activity of a destroyer's bridge. I found that my mind did not take easily to difficult and rapid decisions, with the need at the same time to keep half an ear and half an eye cocked for the unexpected. But it did not help that I had an unpleasant Chief Yeoman (the senior signals rating) who was supposed to be my right-hand man, but who seemed to enjoy watching me make mistakes without correcting me as he should. Finally, my woes were made worse by the fact that my captain was a very experienced signal officer himself, who knew backwards all the answers I had to laboriously look up, and often got not quite right. 'Flags' – the name given to signal officers – 'Surely the right signal group was ABC not ABB?' – 'Why are you routeing this message via Malta not to London direct?' All these things were put right with time – the Chief Yeoman was replaced by a friendly and cooperative one; I eventually learnt my trade; and my captain was replaced by an experienced navigation specialist. Overnight things became quite different. My decisions and advice were not questioned. The Navigating Officer suddenly found he was on the receiving end. "Pilot" – the name given to navigating officers – 'Is this a Fix or a Dead Reckoning?' – 'What were you able to get a fix on?'

-----o0o-----

Like all the Mediterranean Fleet we were based at Malta, at the time a colony, where there was a naval dockyard and all supporting services like stores, ammunition and fuel, and also some excellent sports facilities. Its creeks and harbours provided extensive moorings – Valletta Harbour for large vessels and Sliema Creek and neighbouring inlets for destroyers, minesweepers and submarines. The Headquarters of Commander in Chief, Mediterranean, were also situated in Malta, and his official residence was Admiralty House, Valletta.

Malta was also the home of most families of those serving in the Mediterranean Fleet, as well as many officers who had retired there. For those of us who were still single it provided marvellous recreational opportunities – clubs, restaurants and ballrooms, good cheap car hire, and many pretty girls mostly the daughters of naval officers living locally. *Saintes* and the other ships spent much of their time at Malta on daily exercises and weapon practices, returning to their buoys for the night to give shore leave. For a young officer it was a very nice place to have as a base!

The Duke of Edinburgh, married of course to Princess Elizabeth, was First Lieutenant of HMS *Chequers*, the Leader of the other destroyer squadron of the Mediterranean Fleet, and she often came out to be with him. Whenever this happened destroyers were deployed at intervals along the route of the Royal Flight, so that if the worst happened and the aircraft downed in the sea a rescue ship could be on the scene very soon. We often managed to follow this not very demanding duty with an "operational visit" to one of the French Riviera ports. On one occasion *Saintes* had opted for a visit to Nice. As we reached our scheduled safety position we received a Secret Exclusive from Malta. This meant I had to decode it personally – all Exclusive messages were "officer only" – it read:

'Personal for Captain (D3) from Commander in Chief. For my farewell visit to King Ibn Saud I require a presentation gift of a large bottle of scent with the following characteristics: Pungency. Lurid Colour. Ostentatious Appearance. Grateful if you would obtain this during your visit to Nice.'

On arrival my captain saw the British Consul General and next day he and three of us went in CG's official car to Grasse, not far away, where much of the perfume sold in France is manufactured. We had an interesting tour of one of the factories, emerging smelling like a "whore's boudoir" as the captain put it. We also had with us a medium sized cut glass decanter, full of bright green perfume. We afterwards learnt that the gift had gone down extremely well with the King.

-----oOo-----

Twice a year the Fleet went on cruises, to 'show the flag' to foreign ports, and for exercises. In spring the cruise was usually to the Eastern Mediterranean, and included the Fleet Regatta – sailing and "pulling" contests using the wooden naval boats that every ship carried. For one of these we went to Marmorice

Bay, a large deserted lagoon in Asia Minor, an extinct crater and approached via a long winding channel. The Fleet entered in line ahead, some three miles long, with *Saintes* leading As we approached the entrance we were astonished to find the Turkish flagship – the ancient *Yazouf* – a First World War ex-British battleship anchored bow and stern. As we passed, her sailors in their best white uniforms lined her rails and cheered us. The British fleet was making an informal entry, with sailors all in blue working dress and no ceremonial planned. *Saintes* responded as best we could, and we made an Emergency Signal to the fleet 'Turkish Flagship anchored at lagoon entrance and cheering ship'. By the time the fourth or fifth ship passed the British fleet was organised!

The Turks had other surprises for us. Our regattas were conducted in ship's whalers which were rowed with long oars and sweeping strokes. The Turks had different ideas. Although they had identical boats they rowed with much shorter oars, and at great pace, chopping the water. They lined up clear but abreast of our races, and progressed at a much greater speed. We waved in a friendly sort of way. The *Yazouf* herself was something of a wonder. Some of our dinghies sailed round her. She was moored head and stern, and her starboard side presented to the channel was impeccable, glistening in new grey paint. Not so the port side – untouched and rusty.

There was one more memorable thing about this cruise. As well as major attention being devoted to the Regatta, we had to deal with forest fires. The woods ashore, being Mediterranean summer, were tinder dry. In retrospect unwisely, our sailors were allowed ashore for picnics. Inevitably, of course, fires were started, which joined up to become a huge smouldering conflagration. "Fire Parties" were ordered ashore from every ship, and a considerable proportion of everyone's time was spent in trying to beat it out. To no avail. We left with it still smouldering. Later we heard that settling the bill had cost the British taxpayer a pretty penny.

Not long after this, in the summer of 1951, our squadron had an altogether different task on its hands. In the first of the big post-war Middle East crises, the new Iranian prime minister, Mr Moussadek, decided to nationalise the large oil refinery at Abadan, owned by the British firm then named the Anglo Iranian Oil Company (later BP). This precipitated the "Abadan Crisis", which eventually resulted in major long-term international repercussions. Initially however, the British Government sent the Navy to the rescue.

The Abadan refinery was a huge complex situated near the sea on the banks of the Shatt-al-Arab, the river separating Iran and Iraq – where it was a few hundred metres wide, with the international boundary in the middle. One of the Mediterranean Fleet cruisers was stationed at the port, in Iraqi waters. A squadron of destroyers was also part of the force, with the leader stationed at the port of Basra, in Iraq, some twenty miles upstream. The other destroyer squadron had the first stint of two months, and we relieved them in August. We had been warned it was very hot. As Leader we stopped at an inlet at the Straits of Hormuz at the mouth of the Gulf, for an operational briefing from our predecessor, HMS *Chequers*. As we entered in the late afternoon, we found her at anchor and waiting for us. We soon saw that there was a huge 100 foot long banner stretched all along the "catwalk" – the railed gangway from the funnel to the after castle – held up by their sailors, who were the colour of burnt oak, compared to our nut brown. The banner read:

You'll ABADAN good time!

You'll see everything BAHRAIN
KUWAIT! You'll see what we MINA!

We recognised the first three place names A few days later we entered Mina-al-Ahmedi, a huge anchorage on the coast near Abadan, full of ships waiting to enter port, and so desperately hot that their sailors were beginning to jump overboard in despair. The reader will by now have got the message – it was unbelievably hot! Everyone had to drink at least eight pints of water per day, each accompanied by a large salt pill, to avoid the physical exhaustion of dehydration, and the mental confusion caused by salt deficiency of the blood. The ship's hull became so hot that to avoid burning your feet you had to wear sandals to take a shower. All the ship's cats had to be put down as their pads became blistered.

Saintes spent most of the next few weeks in Basra. There was an operational plan, at a few days' notice, for the army to fly a brigade to Basra, and for our four destroyers to fill up with soldiers and rush them down river to take over Abadan. The chances seemed small to us of surviving such a venture, if the Iranian Army had had any will to fight. The river was only a few hundred yards wide, and was impenetrably lined with palms. A few well-placed field guns, at point-blank range, would have shot our ships to bits. The operation was shortened to four hours' notice for about a week, but at the last moment diplomacy worked, and the whole thing stood down and the Navy pulled out. The eight large tugs at Abadan that berthed and unberthed the tankers had at the start of the crisis been commandeered and taken to Basra with their crews. As our squadron moved downstream we convoyed the tugs to the open sea. As we passed Abadan the huge and unemployed work force was on the half mile long jetty, watching us in silence. It was eerie – the Iranians had got the refinery, but not the port, which could not be worked without tugs. They were watching their livelihood leaving in front of their eyes. A week or so later we stopped for a couple of days at Aden, having cooled off. One of our wardroom remarked that it was wonderful to have three or four proper pees a day again, rather than the occasional puff of steam.

The following spring in 1952 the Fleet went to the large bay at Tobruk. It was only ten years since the North African campaigns of the Second World War, and the port had hardly recovered. The desert outside was littered with landmines, and desolate Bedouin children with missing feet and legs to be seen everywhere. The whole Fleet was at anchor, and one morning, at 'general drill' I was on the bridge, and my Chief Telegraphist called up the voice pipe to report that the Fleet Broadcast, a long range strategic wireless service read by every ship in the Mediterranean, had just passed a message 'Execute to follow – half mast colours'. 'Execute to follow' was a tactical signal, normally used on short range networks to ensure that at the 'Execute' all ships acted together. This was passed, and all ships in company duly half masted their ensigns. Immediately afterwards a further signal was received 'The Board of Admiralty regret to relay the following message issued by Buckingham Palace at 0800 today. "His Majesty King George VI died in his sleep at Sandringham during the night...etc..." The Captain cleared lower deck and made a brief announcement to the ship's company. Work and drills for the day were cancelled. It was a profound shock, quite unexpected. The King and Queen had been a much respected couple.

Princess – now Queen – Elizabeth was in Kenya with her husband the Duke, who broke the news to her. They decided to fly back immediately. The destroyers in Tobruk proceeded at top speed to their safety stations along the flight path. *Saintes* had the longest way to go, and a severe storm was brewing up. It got worse, with the usual short and steep waves that occur in the Mediterranean. We reduced speed, but started to take damage on the fo'c'sle. Eventually we had to "heave to", the only occasion during my career I experienced this extreme measure. The ship never reached its proper position, but fortunately the Royal flight returned home safely.

It was a fitting end to my two years in HMS *Saintes*. Soon afterwards I left the ship to spend my foreign service leave with my parents, who had emigrated to Kenya. I then returned to the UK, to start what became my main work in the Navy – deep specialisation – by taking the year long Advanced Communications Course, known as the Dagger C Course. My service in destroyers was over.

5

Aircraft Carriers

The cheerful looking Rear Admiral paused at the top of the starboard gangway, and the bosuns' calls shrilled their naval welcome as they "piped him over the side". He stepped forward, but instead of extending his right hand he wagged his finger at my Admiral and said, 'Charles, I hear you've been giving parties!' My Admiral was obviously not expecting this, but he laughed, his little goatee beard wagging, 'Come and hear all about it,' he said. They shook hands and went below.

It was the summer of 1959, and HMS *Eagle*, flagship of the Carrier Squadron, had just berthed at head and stern buoys in Valletta Harbour. Our visitor was Rear Admiral Christopher Bonham-Carter, the Chief of Staff to Commander-in-Chief Mediterranean, whose headquarters were in Malta, and he was making his formal call on our arrival. I was Flag Lieutenant to Flag Officer, Aircraft Carriers – Rear Admiral Charles Evans. We had come straight from Naples, where we had indeed given a party, accounts of which had rattled round the Mediterranean Fleet. Amongst other things we had nearly killed the British Consul General, one of the dinner guests who, after an over-indulgent evening, had on leaving precipitated himself head first down the same forty foot gangway that our visitor had just come up. It was certainly the most remarkable party I ever had anything to do with.

But it occurred towards the end of my time in the Aircraft Carriers, a period I shall never forget, and to set it in context I shall have to go back a few years.

-----oOo-----

Aircraft carriers were now the Navy's capital ships, and were quite different from the battleships, cruisers, and destroyers I already knew. They were "platforms" from which aircraft were launched and recovered (very noisily) from their flight decks, housed and maintained when in their huge hangars underneath, and controlled by radar from the carrier's operations rooms when airborne. The personnel onboard fell into two distinct groups – the ship's company, who worked the ship, and the naval air arm personnel (pilots, observers, mechanics etc.) who came and went with their squadrons. There was a distinct but friendly rivalry between the two. Life onboard was run to serve the daily flying programme.

I joined HMS *Centaur* in summer 1954, after my return from Singapore, which I cover in the next chapter. She was the first of the "angled deck" carriers and had been in commission a few months. She was already making naval aviation history, as she carried three revolutionary innovations. This was years before the advent of the "jump jet" and aircraft still had to take off and land at high speed from the flight deck. The "angled deck" meant that aircraft could, if they missed the arrestor wires on touchdown, accelerate and take off again safely, instead of piling into the crash barrier. The new stabilised "mirror sight" gave pilots a continuous and accurate indication of whether they were on their proper landing path, and if not how to correct it – replacing the "batsman" who relied on his personal judgement. Finally the "steam catapult" replaced the hydraulic variety – with its explosive thrust – and provided a smoothly increasing thrust along its length, which allowed heavier planes to be catapult launched.

As a lieutenant commander I was in charge of the Communications Department, but had as assistant a Commissioned Communications Officer, a very experienced ex-lower deck communicator who knew everything that was necessary. I very soon learnt that it was best to leave everything in the technical field to him and my two senior ratings – a Chief Yeoman and a Chief Telegraphist – whilst remaining fully responsible for the overall performance of the department, and for the personnel management of one

Seahawk attempting to land on HMS *Centaur's angled deck, 1954*

and missing ...

of the bigger divisions in the ship. The communications of a carrier are demanding; they include not only the usual radio circuits and message distribution of a large ship, with the extra dimension of the logistics associated with keeping its aircraft fully serviceable, but also the operational networks required for their direct control when airborne. But in this appointment

I soon discovered that as far as the Captain and Commander were concerned it was not my communications duties that concerned them, they assumed that everything would work well. I had two extra-mural duties that were nearer to their hearts.

The first of these was the Ship's Laundry, I was the Laundry Officer. By this time all RN ships had properly equipped laundries, hot and steamy hellholes which were variously manned, either by "Chinese laundry firms" if the ship was on a station anywhere near the Far East, or by volunteers from the ship's company if not. It was all carefully informal – 'ask no questions and you'll get told no lies' – as long as it all worked with no infringement of "naval discipline" the detailed arrangements were left to me. Needless to say, as I was completely unversed in these arts I was dependent on the Petty Officer of the Laundry Party – himself an ex-laundryman. The efficient running of the laundry was vital to the well-being of all onboard, especially in hot weather. I privately gave thanks to the willingness and efficiency of the petty officer and his pirates, and asked very few questions!

My other extra-mural activity I was persuaded to take on was Band Officer. At least in this job I recognised the instruments and most of the music. The RN had greatly run down the Royal Marine Band Service, and ships no longer carried professional bands. They were instead encouraged to form volunteer bands, and could then loan the instruments and music from a central store. Finding competent players was the least of the problems – the nationwide popularity of brass bands provided them in surprising numbers. Moreover I received great support from the Captain, who was extremely keen to parade a band on the flight deck for entering and leaving harbour – when those around us could see, hear and admire, and from the Commander, who was a Scot and President of the RN Pipers Society, and keen on all forms of musical display. He was the source of additional instruments – for example

Blue Jackets Band, HMS *Centaur 1954*

we found ourselves the possessors of a pair of matched tenor drums, rather rare, and not part of the Royal Marine Band repertoire. There were more intractable difficulties. The first was the matter of dress. What was needed was a "blue jackets band", that is all players dressed in traditional sailors' uniform, with sailor hat, striped collar etc. – known as "Square Rig". Junior sailors wore this of course, but petty officers and chiefs, and lesser personnel like cooks and clerks wore "Fore and Aft Rig", with peaked caps and jackets. Although we had several junior sailors as volunteer bandsmen, there were also senior ratings, who did not welcome getting into a dress they had, by hard work, got themselves promoted out of. This problem was surmounted by persuading several officers to join the band; we had a lieutenant commander, who played the euphonium, and two midshipmen volunteered to play the side drums, and they turned out in square rig. The senior ratings were shamed into wearing square rig too.

Another problem was the matter of availability. All members of the band had their normal ships duties to perform, and though releasing them for practice caused little difficulty, parading the full band for entering harbour was another matter. Many senior ratings had duties to perform then as the ship had to be fully prepared for manoeuvring etc. We had one senior engineer rating whose proper duty station was at the main engine throttle control. He played the E flat cornet – a high-pitched small trumpet that provided the flowery descants to many of the better marches. The Ship's Engineer Officer wouldn't release him for entering harbour. The impasse was solved after we paraded the band, less an E flat cornet, and the Captain sent for me and asked what was wrong with the music. I explained. He subsequently had a conversation with the Engineer Officer. The E flat cornet became available to us during all but the most complex of manoeuvres.

Our scope was restricted at first by lack of a professional bandmaster, but we soon got a Band Corporal from the RM Band School, probably because of our impending prestigious Far East cruise. He was splendid, sharpening up the music and the marching, taking practices and giving tuition. He formed a wind octet, which played at mess dinners and for cocktail parties, and actually produced some lovely music. During the cruise we had HMS *Albion* (our sister ship) with us, who also had a blue jackets band, and we paraded massed bands for ceremonies, football matches and the like. They provided a stirring display.

Centaur was a "happy ship", possibly the first aircraft carrier to be so. The dangers inevitably associated with the older carriers (ie not angled deck), with continual accidents and casualties on the flight deck, made for pilots living on their nerves. We had relatively few accidents and fatalities compared with before, and although twice when on watch on the bridge I had personal experience of such harrowing events I will not burden the reader with details. Suffice it to say that they were mercifully few, and as a result we had a wardroom where behaviour was normal, without the heavy drinking previously associated with carrier life. I much enjoyed my time in this ship. Amongst other things I learnt how a carrier works and smells, and how its communications serve it. These were experiences I could not have done without when, some years later, I became Staff Communications Officer to the whole carrier squadron.

-----oOo-----

In early 1958 I joined HMS *Eagle*, flagship of the Carrier Squadron, as Flag Lieutenant and Staff Communications Officer (SCO) to Flag Officer, Aircraft Carriers (FOAC). It was something of a misnomer, as I was now a Lieutenant Commander, but the title "Flag Lieutenant" was sacrosanct. I had come from HMS *Mercury*, the Signal School, where I was one of the senior instructors. My Captain had told me a few months earlier of my next job, and I was very pleased. This was the most sought after seagoing appointment in the Communications Specialisation, and it followed on very nicely from my previous ship HMS *Centaur*. Combining the two roles of flag lieutenant and SCO had its logic, and was still the normal set-up with the main squadron staffs. It meant that the admiral got an experienced officer on his personal staff and someone with good specialisation background for the communications side. I had a junior communications officer as my staff assistant, to whom I could delegate much of the detail, and who could learn much from the appointment himself. But it was a very busy combination as much of one's day was inevitably taken up with the admiral's programme, and attending on him for functions, which of course took precedence, but which meant that what important staff work was properly mine had to be done in the evenings if available, or sandwiched between other matters. Life was never a dull moment.

Eagle was the Navy's premier warship, and had spacious admiral's quarters, right aft on the main deck, comprising a large day cabin or ante-room, a dining room that could sit up to twelve, with galleys and night cabins to match. There were normally five officers in the Admiral's Mess, himself, his Secretary and his Flag Lieutenant, his Chief of Staff, and also the Flag Captain, the

Captain of the ship. My Admiral was Rear Admiral Alexander Bingley. He was an ex-Fleet Air Arm Observer and known throughout the navy as "Baron Bingley", although just why is not clear. He looked the part, craggy and distinguished, but was scathing of what he considered unnecessary fuss: he couldn't stand complexity, wanting to simplify everything. This sometimes made it difficult to get him to agree to the norms of naval etiquette and ceremonial, which was my task to put to him.

In late winter 1959 we sailed from Plymouth to our first port of call, Gibraltar, and a week later made a formal visit to Barcelona. This was in the days of General Franco, the Caudillo of Spain, and everything was closely regulated. A formal visit meant lots of pomp and circumstance; our programme had been carefully arranged by the British Embassy in Madrid, and the Naval Attaché, who spoke Spanish, came down to help with a splendid embassy Rolls Royce to keep our end up. Barcelona is a beautiful city and we had a most enjoyable visit, but what I remember most were our official calls. It took us a whole day to make them, and another to receive the return calls on board. Barcelona is the regional capital of Catalonia, and this meant seven calls in all, in strict pecking order, each accompanied by the appropriate welcome. First on the City Mayor, then the Chief of Police followed by the Regional Council. These being civilian organisations, no guards or bands. Then the National Police, or Guarda Civilia – a uniformed and drilled detachment greeted us in their distinctive uniforms. Then the three services, with increasingly imposing ceremonial. The Air Force, being the least in pecking order, mounted a normal guard and small band; then the Navy, a large guard, ensigns, and a large band. Finally the Captain General, in command (no less) of the Region and second only to Franco in national ranking. There was no mistaking the message. A huge armed guard – a whole company it seemed – wearing shiny round black helmets, the whole formation flanked by two small tanks. Flags and emblems. No band (too effeminate?) but a fanfare of bugles.

The other notable event in Barcelona was an unexpected visitor one evening. A smart cruise liner (rare vessels in those days, and only for the rich) docked in the port, when the Admiral, discovering that friends of his were onboard, invited them for evening drinks. An excited message arrived in reply, 'May we bring Noel Coward too as he has just joined us?' *Eagle* was at anchor off the port of Barcelona, and I went in with the barge to pick them up. Noel Coward was instantly recognisable. He was older than I expected and very fulsome. He sat on the barge's cushions looking forward as we returned to the ship. 'Lovely to be back with the Navy again,' he intoned, obviously reminding us of his part in the wartime film *In Which We Serve*. As it was a purely private party the Admiral had not suggested I join them, so I had supper in my cabin and got down to some staff work instead.

From Barcelona we proceeded – via the inevitable exercises en route, the Navy never went anywhere together without exercising at something – to Malta. Antonia and I had been married during my previous appointment at the Signal School and she came out to be with me whilst the ship was there. Her brother John, a Royal Marine officer, and his wife Sarah were based in Malta, and as it happened went back to England for a few weeks. They lent us their flat for the short time *Eagle* was in port – a splendid break for us. Alas, it was all too short, because a week or so later the Middle East erupted into another of its periodic crises, with the revolution and bloody end of the ruling dynasty in Iraq. This eventually led to the rise of Sadam Hussein, but immediately it meant that the Kingdom of Jordan was under threat. The UK had close ties with Jordan, and a token force of a few hundred troops was flown out to the capital Amman, to act as a deterrent to any attempt at invasion. To give this credibility the British Government decided to keep a small combat air patrol of fighters at immediate notice to support them, and this task fell on the Navy's carriers.

The operational need was for one carrier to be on station, and the range of naval fighters at that date meant that it had to be off the coast in the eastern Mediterranean. This needed escorts, destroyers or frigates, to deter any attempt at sneak attack, and since all ships had to be at sea for weeks if necessary the force had to have replenishment vessels (oilers and supply ships) in the form of Royal Fleet Auxiliaries (RFAs) In all this amounted to a considerable force, and in later years it would have been called a Task Force. FOAC became the Force Commander. As SCO it was my job to devise and promulgate the Communications Plan for the "Eastern Mediterranean Force" as it was named. This was not terribly complicated, but we were effectively at war stations and it was important that everything should work smoothly and provide an instant response if necessary. Long range radio communications were still provided by High Frequency (HF) circuits, which were of low capacity, and prone to unreliability. During an operation of this nature communications traffic increased enormously due to the need for extra operational signals and reports, and this often required the Admiralty to issue the order "Minimize" amplified by the area concerned. When ordered only operational and very urgent administrative signals were sent by radio, and the rest by mail the delays being accepted. Sure enough, before long FOAC had to request "Minimize Eastern Mediterranean", which did the trick.

As soon as the Iraq crisis broke *Eagle* sailed for Cyprus, where the UK still had a "sovereign base area" at Akrotiri, where we relieved our sister ship HMS *Ark Royal*, which was due home for refit. I should explain that the Navy was still in the position that its ships and their equipment needed regular dockyard support in one form or another, from deep refit to "extended maintenance". This was greatly improved over the years, which led to the position some twenty years later of the Falklands Task Force being continuously at sea for months in the South Atlantic. However, in 1958 it meant a regular rotation of vessels between our operational area and Malta. It also meant that the carrier on station, the lynch pin of the operation, regularly had to be relieved by another of the squadron. This entailed FOAC "shifting his flag" and taking several of his operational staff with him to the new carrier, which meant splitting the staff and much extra communication as a result. As a consequence it was a very busy time for us all, in particular for me as the Staff Communicator, but with practically nothing to do as Flag Lieutenant. This situation lasted most of the rest of the year, until the crisis was resolved, and *Eagle*, with the flag back on board, returned to Plymouth for Christmas, where we all took some welcome leave.

-----o0o-----

I returned to *Eagle* in January 1959 after a very pleasant Christmas break, to find that my admiral had been promoted, and was as a consequence now a Vice Admiral. He was also going to be relieved, and the rumour (not to be discussed, but confirmed soon after) was that he was going to relieve my previous admiral – Sir Charles Lambe – as C-in-C Mediterranean. (Charles Lambe then came home to be First Sea Lord). "Baron Bingley" left his flagship a week or so later, true to form to the end. The officers of HMS *Eagle*, staff and ship, proposed sending him off in what had become something of a time-honoured tradition in the RN, towing his car away on the jetty with two long tow ropes. He objected, as usual, protesting it was "too much fuss", but was persuaded to accept as a mark of respect from what was certainly his last seagoing command. He got the last laugh. He ordered his driver to put the hand brakes on as soon as the tow began, and it all ground to a standstill. 'Come on lads!' shouted the Chief of Staff, who was in charge of the tow, 'Let's show the Admiral what we can do.' We were about forty all told, and we set to as if we were two tug-of-war teams. The car with the admiral inside was slithered, its tyres protesting, for about thirty yards before we gave up. The ropes were undone, and we cheered him away as he drove off laughing.

My new boss, Rear Admiral Charles Evans, was a quite different personality. He was a well-known ex-Fleet Air Arm Pilot, rather dapper with a little beard, very affable, and with a courtly manner – whereas "The Baron", though friendly, was often very taciturn. Charles Evans and I got on very well, and it helped that by now I had the measure of my rather busy job. He was a great entertainer. One of our first ports of call was at Gibraltar for the 1959 Home Fleet Spring Assembly, exercises on the way there, and Fleet Sports and Fleet Boxing Tournament whilst in port. The Commander-in-Chief, Home Fleet was there flying his flag in his headquarters' ship, HMS *Tyne* a converted submarine tender. This was in the days when the last of the battleships, HMS *Vanguard*, was in the Reserve Fleet, and the idea that the C-in-C's Headquarters might be ashore – as it eventually was at Northwood – was quite foreign. He was of course the most senior officer present, but on this occasion was outranked by the First Lord of the Admiralty, Mr J.P.Thomas, who was there in the C-in-C's despatch vessel – a converted minelayer. The First Lord was a well-known *bon viveur*, and Charles Evans had the brilliant idea of inviting him to lunch, and for the three of us, with me as Flag Lieutenant driving the admiral's official car, to have a proper Spanish meal at a well-known slap-up restaurant on the other side of the Bay of Gibraltar. It was a Sunday, and I booked the table for three for 1 o'clock. It wouldn't matter if we were a bit late, as Spanish hours were well behind British ones, and the only other engagement the First Lord had that day was a big dinner party hosted by the Commander in Chief in *Tyne*.

Being Sunday morning, there were one or two engagements first: Church in the Cathedral, drinks with the Dean afterwards, and a quick visit to the Nurses Quarters for a pre-lunch snifter. We should with luck get to the restaurant at 1 o'clock. But it didn't turn out quite like that. Church was OK, and the drinks at the Dean's lasted only a little longer than planned. But the nurses were very hospitable, and the First Lord much enjoyed their hospitality. Despite promptings from me, we only got on the road for Spain at 2 o'clock. We arrived at the restaurant at 3 o'clock, but of course that was normal timing for Spanish lunch, and the Admiral and the First Lord enjoyed a couple of glasses of sherry while they took pains to order their meal, which then had to be cooked. We finally sat down well after 4 o'clock. By this time I had started to "heel tap" but while they were having their coffee and brandy the band started up. 'Now I really do like the Spanish habit of producing a band for the lunch time brandies exclaimed the First Lord. It was 7 o'clock and the band had come on for the evening. I started to make even more determined signs to the Admiral that we *had* to go. I paid the bill, and we clambered into the car, which I drove at breakneck for the border. We got to the First Lord's despatch vessel at 8 o'clock after a furious drive, to find his "minder", the First Lieutenant of the ship and normally very unflappable, waiting by the gangway looking distinctly worried. The Commander in Chief's dinner guests, who included the Governor of Gibraltar, had been asked at "7.45 for 8.0" but they couldn't sit down until the First Lord of the Admiralty, a Cabinet Minister and the guest of honour, had arrived. We put him onboard his vessel and the First Lieutenant got to work, getting him changed into his white tie etc. He finally got to HMS *Tyne* only an hour or so late.

-----o0o-----

That summer produced the usual round of exercises, short periods in Malta, and very nice longer periods based on Akrotiri Bay in Cyprus, with lovely bathing and interesting trips ashore to see some of that beautiful island's sights. The Navy was still keeping one carrier in the eastern Mediterranean, available in case of further trouble but not actually at the ready. Then in late summer we went to Naples for an informal visit, where *Eagle* anchored in the Bay just off the port. In the scale of importance of ship visits this was not as grand as that one to Barcelona, nor would it have been as Italy was a NATO ally with whom we had close ties already, as opposed to Spain which at the time was still a dictatorship and at arm's length.

But it was much more than an operational visit, when there would have been no ceremony or official entertaining and calls were considered paid and returned. Caserta, just outside Naples was the huge headquarters of Commander in Chief, NATO Southern Command, a principal military region of the Alliance and encompassing all the Mediterranean and most of its littoral ports. The C-in-C was a four-star American Admiral in command not only of NATO forces in his area but also in national command of the US Sixth Fleet. His post was one of the most senior in the US and NATO, and he was obviously top of our list for calls. He was a universally popular figure, and he and his wife were the principal guests at the dinner party that Charles Evans decided to give on board *Eagle*. This of course was 'The Party' alluded to at the beginning of this chapter.

At first sight it should have been no problem. Dinner for twelve, white tie or equivalent; the guest list agreed with the British Embassy in Rome and the Naval Attaché and his wife included to help with the Italian Fleet Commander, the other main guest, who spoke little English. The remaining guests were the British Consul General, Naples – who also spoke Italian – and his wife.

The first thing that went slightly wrong was that the Italian Admiral arrived in his barge at the port gangway. The port and starboard gangway spaces in a large carrier are not directly interconnected, and in accordance with naval custom the entire welcoming party was assembled at the starboard gangway. He was received on board by a surprised midshipman of the watch, and ushered round, just as our barge was coming alongside with the other guests.

We got over that one and the party assembled in the Admiral's day cabin for pre-dinner drinks. It soon became evident that we had a problem with the Consul General. He had just arrived in Naples, having been transferred from another city, where he had had to be "dried out" before resuming duties, but was understood to be fine now. He had just married again, and it became obvious that he had fortified his nerves well before setting out, and that he was *very* fond of his new wife, who did not seem to mind him making this apparent to all. But drinks proceeded and we soon sat down. The Italian Admiral was fairly uncommunicative, but the NA and his wife were alongside and opposite him and conversed in Italian. The American admiral (I will call him Admiral White) was charming and courteous. Mrs White was believed to be hooked, but not noticeably so, on something stronger than "the weed". That night however she was obviously feeling amorous and the Flag Captain and the Chief of Staff, who were seated on either side of her, discovered later that at one point they had each been holding a clutching hand.

The Consul General had had plenty of further support before dinner, and was by now very much the worse for wear. He sat slumped in his seat and only conversed when spoken to. The Naval Attaché and I were sitting alongside each other and we quietly hatched a plan for what to do if he actually collapsed. He and I would drag CG next door, and get him onto a stretcher and onto a bunk in one of night cabins, where we would get a ship's doctor to attend to him. But this wasn't necessary; he got through the meal without mishap. After the port had been passed and the toasts been drunk Mrs Attaché "gathered the ladies" and they withdrew for coffee. CG suddenly realized that his wife was not present. He stood up and addressed his host. 'Admiral,' he said, 'I'm afraid I shall have to leave you. I've lost my wife.' He was persuaded that all was well and sat down, and shortly after we joined the ladies for the brandy and liqueurs.

The Italian Admiral's barge arrived (at the port gangway again); he insisted on going immediately and the Flag Captain saw him off. Our barge was brought alongside the starboard gangway for the remaining guests who gathered on deck. Mrs White persuaded me to go down first with her and we sat in the barge's cabin, where she tried to show me her affection.

The Naval Attaché and his wife started down, followed by the CG's wife. Admiral White as senior guest was due to leave last, so it was CG's turn. He stood stiffly to attention at the top of the ladder and addressed Charles Evans. 'Admiral,' he said, 'It's been a wonderful party. Thank you so much.' He bowed from the waist, and went on bowing. He shot, head first, right the way from top to bottom of the forty foot ladder, brushing past the three startled guests on the way down. There was a terrific clatter, and he landed in a crumpled heap on the bottom platform. I bounded out of the barge's cabin and wondered what to do. He was obviously badly injured or worse, and I wasn't sure if it was safe to try and move him, as his back or neck were probably broken. I looked up, to see a line of astonished faces (Admiral, Flag Captain, Chief of Staff etc.) looking over the rail, goggle eyed and mouths all open, presuming he was dead. As I bent over him he opened an eye and looked at me. Very slowly he got up. His stiff shirt was crumpled, his bow tie askew, and he had a small scratch on his left cheek, as if he had nicked himself shaving. He stood up, shakily. 'I think I must have missed my footing,' he said.

He had of course illustrated the truth of the myth that, if you are drunk enough a fall will result in a soft landing. Admiral White joined us, the barge took us ashore, and they got into their respective cars and drove off. We afterwards heard that CG had spent the next three days in bed, "somewhat bruised". We never heard any more, although I can't imagine that there were no repercussions; after all the Naval Attaché went back to Rome and must have let the Ambassador know of it all. But *Eagle* left for Malta the next day, and as far as we were concerned that was the end of it.

The final significant episode in my time in the carriers were the 1959 Autumn Exercises, which occurred every two years and simulated a carrier task force steaming from Gibraltar towards the UK and launching air strikes, with opposition provided by the RAF. FOAC was Force Commander, and we decided to evaluate whether it would be beneficial to arrange formations of ships at sea so that the patterns they presented to aircraft radars did not immediately identify the picture as a naval force. It was extremely successful, and lead within two years to major changes in NATO naval tactical doctrine.

My time in the Carrier Squadron had come to an end, and as I had much to do with the devising of these new techniques I was not surprised to find myself as one of the exercise analysis team which reported its findings three months later, a task I found most interesting. I then joined the instructional staff at the Navigation and Direction School, HMS *Dryad*, near Portsmouth, teaching "electronic warfare". Both these appointments meant that Antonia and I could continue to live at our home nearby. Together they lasted only a year or so, and I then received the glad news that I had been selected for promotion to Commander. But I had been placed on the "dry list", which meant that my seagoing days were over. I had mixed feelings, as it was a pang to find I would no longer serve in ships. But I was becoming very interested in my specialisation, and in retrospect it was clearly the right way forward for me. My career as a communications specialist would continue as a staff officer ashore.

Part Two

ASHORE

… when Thou givest Thy servant
the undertaking of any great matter,
grant that he may understand
that it is not the beginning
but the continuing of the same
until it be thoroughly finished
that yieldeth the true glory.

(Drake's Prayer)

6

Naval Signals

'So you see, from now on you need never work in the afternoon.' Twelve pairs of drooping eyes looked up. This was something they had not heard before. It was the last day of a year-long course in naval communications, the Long C Course, and they were within minutes of being told, they hoped, that they had passed their final exams and were qualified specialists. The previous evening they had been the guests at the Mess Dinner at the Signal School, hence the drooping eyes. That morning they had listened to a series of predictable farewell addresses from their senior instructors. The next and final speaker was the Captain of the Signal School, who would tell them not only the glad news, but also their first appointments as signal officers.

The speaker suggesting this unlikely life of ease was the Executive Officer of the establishment. His job was purely administrative, and he had played no part in their instruction – in fact it would probably have been beyond him. He was one of an old breed of signal officer, a rapidly dying species, who regarded technical detail as something to be left to subordinates. They were usually rich and well-connected: he was an 'Hon' and his predecessor had been a belted earl. He explained his point. You attended to matters affecting the communications department in the morning, discussed things with your senior ratings, and made any decisions needed. Once a week you carried out departmental rounds and suchlike, but by midday you were free. Afternoons could be spent playing polo or golf or whatever. It took us very little time in our new posts to discover how wrong he was.

It was now spring 1950, and it had been a very pleasant year at HMS *Mercury*, the Signal School, at Leydene House on the Hampshire downs near Petersfield, with views of the Isle of Wight and as far as the New Forest. The instruction had not been over-demanding, and had not prevented us from enjoying the delights of Hampshire society. For young officers who had spent the last five years or more in ships, this was a luxury. The course had taught us much, sending and reading Morse, ordering and interpreting flag hoists and manoeuvring signals; learning how radio equipment worked, known as "Technical", and how to use it to create networks, known as "Organisation". We were introduced to the mysteries of cyphers, and the still secret world of electronic warfare. Since signal officers were frequently appointed as an admiral's flag lieutenant, the equivalent of ADC, we learnt the intricacies of naval ceremonial, the protocol of table plans for dinner parties, and how to arrange the admiral's personal programme. Looking back now, we were probably taught too much. Nowadays similar specialists are trained in far less time.

Our instructors were carefully selected for their posts and very knowledgeable in their particular fields. This was in 1949, so we had the advantage of being taught by people who had war experience. At the time we hardly noticed it – everyone had served in the war. But they believed that the lessons that signal officers had learnt the hard way should be passed on to the next generation. Perhaps the most important of these was that the communications plan for an operation *had* to be developed as part of the general plan, not tacked on at the end when it might be found that what was needed was not possible and the whole plan necessarily reworked.

This is the place to ask, 'Why specialise?' For me the only alternative was *not* to specialise, and thus be known as a "salt horse". Such officers were rather rare, and becoming more so, and represented those who did not want to specialise. Some thought they could not master the technicalities. Others were aggressively "seamen", preferring the ship side of naval life – bridge and upper deck work, ropes, anchors and cables etc. More importantly one was more likely to be promoted as a specialist. I had always assumed I would specialise – my father had been a gunnery officer, and hoped I would follow him. In his young days the 'big gun' had reigned supreme, and the gunnery specialisation was seen as the tops. But the war had changed all that and the dominant naval weapon was the carrier borne aircraft. I flirted with becoming a naval Pilot, but eventually changed my preference to Communications. (I must explain that the terms "signals" and "communications" meant, at that time, much the same thing in the Navy.) During my Subs Courses I had been very interested to learn how ships were manoeuvred by tactical signals and how signal officers, when on the bridges of admirals and commodores, were their advisers on such matters. I also liked the way in which Signal Officers seemed to belong to a club – all knowing each other and very friendly. This led to my joining the Long Communications Course, usually referred to as one's Long Course, in 1949, a career move which I have never regretted.

Specialisation has always featured in navies, as indeed in most other walks of life. Historically, although the captain commanded the ship, the Master was in charge of the set of the sails and the steering. The Master Gunner ordered the loading of the guns and controlled their fire. As steam replaced sail, Engineers were required, and Seamen were joined by Stokers. With time and new weapons the RN acquired Torpedomen, Submariners, and Pilots, and of course Signal Officers. New specialisations were only introduced when absolutely necessary. For many years the ship's electrics were the responsibility of the Torpedo Branch, and the new fangled wireless sets belonged to the Telegraphists, and thus to the Signal Branch. During the Second World War rapid technical advances spawned new specialisations, and following the war those covering all forms of electrical, radio and radar equipment were amalgamated into the Electrical Branch. The distinction was made between "users" and "maintainers", the electricians being responsible for the onboard repair and maintenance of communications equipment, and the communicators (the new jargon for signal officers, telegraphists, and signalmen) for operation. It took time for this to settle down, but with subsequent minor adjustments this set up lasted during my communications career.

A friendly senior officer once pointed out to me that one's early career was usually concerned with operating the *current* Navy – doing the necessary in ships and staffs, training officers and men etc. – but that as one rose in rank, particularly as a specialist, one became more engaged with the *future* navy – deciding what was needed in the way of new ships and equipment, and supervising their introduction, for which it was necessary to have complete grasp of how the current navy worked. This was very much the pattern of my career; I learnt my trade as a communicator in ships and staffs until promotion to the rank of commander. Thereafter I became mostly involved with planning the introduction of the next generation of communications systems.

Following the Long Course my first job as a communicator was as Staff Communications Officer to the 3rd Destroyer Squadron. On return to the UK I was not surprised to find that I had been nominated for the Advanced Communications Course – or Dagger C Course as it was known, as one's entry in the Navy List was as a "dagger specialist" with the abbreviation C†. My Captain had sent for me and said that the qualification was being reintroduced, and asked if I would like to be considered for it. I had said yes, and realized I would be a likely choice, as I had come near the top in my Long Course, and had done well in technical subjects.

Pre-war the signals specialization had had Dagger C's, who dealt with the detail of radio equipment, but it had lapsed and there were effectively none left. This left something of a problem, as there were now no communications officers left with sufficient understanding of what was needed as a course curriculum, or how best to select candidates. They were therefore in the hands of the academic staff at the Royal Naval College Greenwich, where all dagger courses were held, and who "over-egged" the syllabus (not least probably because they had their own jobs in mind too). As a consequence we found we were being taught not only radio amplification and wave propagation, for example, which we did need, but also ballistics and metallurgy, which we didn't. There were two signal officers on the first course, and we teamed up with the Dagger G's (gunnery) where the courses coincided. I found it difficult but possible, but I am afraid my companion found it all too difficult. He was clearly a misfit, but after a month or so very conveniently found he was required to be seconded to the Foreign Office for some highly secret work, and left Greenwich, so faces were saved all round. The course lasted a full academic year, but it was obvious to me that it could without damage be pruned to two terms only. I enjoyed my time on the course, which allowed one to get up to London without difficulty. It spanned the 1953 Coronation, a splendid event, and we watched the procession from my father's London club overlooking Pall Mall.

Greenwich College offered a wide choice of sports, including athletics. I took up sprinting again (having been a successful sprinter at Dartmouth) and eventually won the Nore Command sprint championships. My brother Stephen, three years my junior and still in the Navy then, similarly won the Naval Air Command championships, and as consequence we both found ourselves representing the Navy in the Tri-Service Athletics. I don't know of any other occasion of two brothers doing the same.

-----oOo-----

On completion of the Dagger Course I found myself appointed to the Staff of Commander in Chief Far East Station in Singapore. I travelled out "grey funnel" as it was known, in a RN vessel used as a trooper. She was HMS *Perseus*, a small Second World War carrier with a greatly reduced crew and no operational capability as a result, but with huge capacity for naval passengers, stores, and of course spare aircraft, all for delivery abroad. It was a sensible use of ships in reserve, as it saved the costs of commercial troopers and freighters, and kept the ships in good condition if they were required to be returned to the Fleet. One of the many passengers on board was an admiral who had just come from a spell of duty in the Admiralty, who was on his way to take up the post of Head of Service of the Indian Navy (they did not yet have sufficiently senior Indian officers). He asked me to give him some tuition on naval communications, which I was pleased to do as the trip provided little meaningful occupation. It was during these spells with him that I first learnt of the Navy's problems with the matter of sea time for officers. It had been decided, as the size of the Fleet diminished, to ration the increasingly rare appointments available for sea command, as high ranking officers had to have sea experience behind them. This led in a year or so to the introduction of the so called "wet" and "dry" lists, with officers promoted to commander on one or other, which had a profound effect on my own career.

I found Singapore surprisingly hot and sticky. It was on the equator, weather varied little during the year, and each day had its tropical downpour. As a child I had visited the place, but had no recollection of all this. Europeans who lived there became accustomed to it after a few weeks, and as a result became naturally lazy – nature's defence presumably. At first one was rather critical of them giving in so easily, and at first I continued to wash my car myself as usual. But after a month or two I found it was preferable to get a grateful coolie to do it for few coins. The torrential rain storms were remarkably local, and you could often see the line of rain across the road as the storm moved slowly along. To prove this I once stopped my car just after I had entered a storm and reversed into the dry, before resuming my journey in rain. The heat had remarkable effects on plant life – for instance gardenias grew like weeds.

The job was interesting but not demanding. I was assistant to a commander who was Fleet Communications Officer, who became a personal friend for many years. The work involved ensuring that the communications organisation serving the far-flung station, which extended from the Indian Ocean to Hong Kong, Japan and beyond, worked efficiently, and where necessary occasionally "tweaking it".

Singapore was a very pleasant place for a bachelor, lots of young people of both sexes, and excellent and cheap restaurants, clubs and swimming pools, and opportunities to picnic and bathe from the small islands close by in the Straits of Malacca. This was when I had my salad days! The place had had a very nasty war under Japanese occupation, and there were plenty of gruesome stories of what had happened in Changi Jail, but the local population were determined to put it all behind them. Culture, too, was arriving; there was an excellent local music society, with its own large choir which I joined, which produced first-class music, completely cosmopolitan with British, Dutch, Malayan and Indian players and singers. I particularly remember a magnificent performance of the *St Matthew Passion* in the Cathedral, for which top class soloists were flown out from Europe. All in all I thoroughly enjoyed my two years in the post.

-----oOo-----

My most vivid memories of my time in Singapore, however, are of the Commander in Chief himself, Admiral Sir Charles Lambe. He was a charismatic figure; of such a reputation that news of his impending arrival would precede him to a new command, to send a "frisson" through all ranks. He had already had a notable career in the Navy, and was a lifelong friend of Lord Mountbatten, who had returned to complete his career in the Navy after retiring from the position of the last Viceroy of India. Charles Lambe had a wide variety of friends in top places in the Arts and in politics, which he extended markedly in the cosmopolitan society of Singapore. He had a spectrum of interests and abilities – he was an accomplished pianist, who had sung in the Bach Choir for many years, a keen bird watcher and photographer, he sketched and painted, and embroidered for relaxation. If anyone deserved the description "polymath" it was Charles Lambe.

He had married late, to a charming and artistic lady who brought her own young son to the marriage, and Charles and Peta then added their own children. It was a difficult set up, and took up much of his time. I always said that he spent one third of his energy on helping his family, another third on his widespread interests, and the final third on running his command. The last he achieved by adopting that much admired – but not always accomplished – art of effective delegation. He listened carefully to every problem, analysed it, took the necessary decisions and then left the implementation to his subordinates. He was a good chooser of men, and had an extremely competent Chief of Staff.

I became personally involved with Charles Lambe and his family when his Flag Lieutenant had to take leave to deal with his father's affairs after his death – he had been a tea planter in Malaya. Charles Lambe sent for me and asked me to be a temporary replacement, accepting that my staff job would have to be mostly left vacant for the period. I moved into the flag lieutenant's quarters in Admiralty House, a palatial residence in the equivalent of "millionaires' row" in the outskirts of the city. I found that my training on my Long Course had provided me with all I needed, and Charles himself couldn't have been easier to serve. I attended on the Admiral when he was away from the office, organised with his approval his official dairy of events, and produced his daily programme. Parties at Admiralty House were discussed with Lady Lambe, and I effectively became one of the family, announcing visitors, where necessary, at parties, and then helping with the details. I remember one scintillating dinner party for all the soloists

Admiral Sir Charles Lambe

who had come out for the *St Matthew Passion*, two of whom were staying as guests in Admiralty House. After dinner they had a bravura sing-song, with Charles at the piano. Without music they sang impromptu from memory – solos, duets, and quartets from operas, musicals etc.

Some months later, after the Flag Lieutenant had returned and I had gone back to my normal duties, living in the Staff Mess, the Lambes were going to be away for several weeks on an official tour. Charles Lambe asked me if I minded (!) moving into the flag lieutenant's quarters at Admiralty House (all found etc) as he didn't trust the Chinese Chief Steward not to take advantage of an empty house. I had a really cushy existence for a few weeks. He also took me with him as his Cypher Officer several times when away in his despatch vessel on official visits, where Lady Lambe insisted (somewhat to my embarrassment – but delight) that I should move from the Wardroom and join them in the Admiral's Quarters and become the "spare flag lieutenant" to help with parties.

Charles Lambe gilded the lily of what was a wonderful time of my life. My admiration for him was shared with many others; he eventually became the only officer to hold four of the top positions in the Navy – C-in-C Far East, Second Sea Lord, C-in-C Mediterranean, and First Sea Lord.

On my return from Singapore my next job was in HMS *Centaur,* following which I joined the teaching staff at HMS *Mercury,* the Signal School near Petersfield, in charge of radio instruction for officers and men. The supervisory aspects of the job were relatively minor, as most things were already up and running and only needed minor attention. My principal teaching task was Course Officer to the Long Courses. The details I already knew backwards, but it meant much time preparing lecture notes, and setting and marking exams, as well as time actually spent in the classroom.

An equally demanding task was commenting on innumerable files sent down from the Signal Division in the Admiralty, for 'the opinion of the Signal School'. This had become standard practice for their staff when dealing with complex matters of communications policy. They lacked the time, and often the expertise, for such subjects, and the Signal School obligingly helped "for free". It was obviously not the best way to deal with such matters, and whilst I was there the beginnings of how to do it better were put in hand. The other major specialist schools (Gunnery, Torpedoes, Navigation and Direction) all had their own 'X' Sections, as they were called, small staffs that served their parent Divisions in Admiralty, and which dealt in an organised way with much of the detail of future policy. For historic reasons, largely because it was only formed during the Second World War, the Signal School never had such an appendage, and absorbed the work load without complaint. It was very inefficient and understaffed, and eventually we got our own 'X' Section. Meanwhile, however, I was able, amongst many other things, to recommend Admiralty approval for the names of communications ratings to be changed. The terms "Telegraphist" and "Signalman" were by now completely anachronistic: Both branches used voice radio, and other forms of radio communication were rapidly being introduced. All communicators became "Radio Operators", a term already in use in the merchant navy which everyone understood.

-----oOo-----

The first few months at the Signal School were my final bachelor days. The other little thing I did during my time there was to get married! Antonia and I met in the autumn of 1956, and after a whirlwind courtship got engaged on Christmas Eve. We were married in May 1957, and my brother Stephen, who had joined the Church, and Elizabeth were married a few weeks later. My parents had emigrated to Kenya and made a family settlement of their affairs in the UK, as a result of which I became the owner of the family house and its surroundings.

On return from honeymoon Antonia and I moved in. It was less than half an hour's drive to work.

The place, in particular the roof, was in very poor repair. But it was summer and the place was no problem. That winter, however, the roof finally became impossible – the lead on the extensive flats had crystallized. Leaks everywhere; and at one stage I counted seventeen buckets and chamber pots catching the drips and dribbles. Next summer we patched the roof up and made it tolerable. Antonia and I decided to get on with completing the unfinished conversion of seventy-odd years earlier, and make the place easier to run as a family home. After what was a considerable programme lasting several years, which meant scrimping and saving and selling some valuable possessions, the house looked normal, and the internal improvements made it comfortable. Our children duly arrived and the place became our family home. It had a large garden, and we kept cats and donkeys.

In early 1958 my time at the Signal School was up, but I was very pleased to hear that my next job was to be in HMS *Eagle* on the carrier squadron staff. Our family had not yet arrived, so Antonia was able to come down to Devonport for the periods that the ship was in port there, and also fly out to Malta for a short time too. In summer 1959 I was selected for promotion to Commander.

7

Washington D.C.

On promotion to commander in summer 1961, I was appointed to the Signal School HMS *Mercury* again, as Training Commander and later as Commander X. I greatly enjoyed these two years at HMS *Mercury* – which are part of the next chapter – not least because it meant that Antonia and I could continue to live at our home nearby. But in late 1962 I was told that my next job was to be Staff Communications Officer on the British Naval Staff, Washington. As with many officers so appointed, I would first take the six months US Joint Staff Course – that is with officers of all three services as students – in Norfolk, Virginia, and then go to Washington on completion. The job was to be "accompanied", that is Antonia and our family, plus Josephine their nanny would come too. We already had our first two children, Katherine and Robin, but Robin our second was too young to travel into the extreme heat of a Virginia high summer. So I preceded the family by two months.

-----oOo-----

I joined the Armed Forces Staff College, Norfolk, Virginia, in mid-July 1963, and as I was on my own I lived in the Officers' Mess until Antonia and the family arrived. The college was run on logical American lines. There were 240 students, arranged into 16 groups for instruction, known as "seminars" each one composed of five officers from each of the three US services, plus one "oddball" student. The latter were from NATO armed forces and US Government departments other then Defence – such as State Department, CIA etc. This mix was intended to ensure that the American officers realized that there were other points of view than their own.

I learnt much at the AFSC, perhaps not so much about staff work, which after all was based on American methods and procedures, but a lot about the US armed forces themselves, and America in general. In particular I learnt to understand the Americans' problems with size of their forces, and how they dealt with them. They had learnt the hard way in the Second World War of the difficulties of moving and supplying large scale amphibious operations in the Pacific, and army groups in Europe. The lessons learnt had provided detailed procedures for the measurement of what was needed and how it should be moved. In fact, it sometimes seemed to the foreign students on course that the ability to mount adequate logistics had become more important than the actual combat operations they supported!

Antonia, Katherine, Robin and Josephine joined me in September, and we occupied a little house, close to the naval air base and very noisy. I had rented it before they came, and was determined not to live on too grand a scale for the remaining months of the course, so as to leave what money was available to get into a proper home in Washington. Moving cash between UK and USA was virtually impossible (dollar area etc.) and one was therefore dependent on the generous foreign living allowance from the RN, but this was paid monthly, and one couldn't spend too much moving in without getting into debt. It needed careful planning. A month or so later came the dreadful matter of the death of President Kennedy. Like everyone else, I remember it all vividly, in particular the pictures of Jacqueline Kennedy returning to Washington with her clothes still covered in blood.

In early spring 1964 we moved to Washington, and life looked up. Antonia and I had visited the city at Christmas and found our next home, not where we had expected amongst American officers in Virginia, but an old fashioned wooden house in a wooded area in the NW section of Washington DC, quite close to the Embassy and full of American civilian families – many of whom became long-term friends. We rented it at a good rate, and were very happy in it – perhaps the best measure of its suitability was that it was taken over in turn by the next three incumbents in my job.

I was a member of the British Naval Staff, Washington (BNS), whose offices were in part of the US Navy buildings overlooking Potomac Park near the Lincoln Memorial, of Second World War vintage and soon to be demolished. However, my office was in the modern building of the British Embassy, a mile or so away up Massachusetts Avenue, where I was accommodated with the remainder of the UK service communicators (i.e. Army, Air Force and Defence). My principal job was to represent the Director of Naval Signals in his relationship with his US Naval equivalent. The ties between the British and American services were as strong as ever. They had never been completely closed down after the end of the Second World War, when the machinery of cooperation between the two nations' Chiefs of Staff, based in Washington, had been established by Roosevelt and Churchill. It had continued quietly, and now that the Cold War was on it was being used to the full. Tactical cooperation between the RN and USN was the lynch pin of the concept of naval operations for NATO; and the mobility of naval forces made the interoperability of RN/USN communications essential. In the Pacific War the two navies had worked together closely, and formations could often include ships from either nation. But advances in technology were beginning to make this difficult, and potentially impossible – the Americans were already years ahead of us, and simple procedural adjustments no longer provided an easy solution.

About five years earlier the two navies had agreed at high level to establish a planning organisation named 'NAVCOMS', to which the two navies, plus the Canadian Navy (and later the Australians too) belonged. This provided that the three Directors of Naval Signals, known as the Navcoms Board, would meet once a year with their supporting staffs and review the whole matter of interoperability between their navies, now and into the future, and then make a written report to the three First Sea Lords. The very fact that this happened sharpened everyone's minds. The cog that drove the machine was a small group of communication specialists from the three navies, all based in Washington, which met once a fortnight to process papers from all navies, amalgamate them into reports and proposals, and generally guide the Board, and provide policy papers for agreement at the yearly meeting. This was called the Permanent Steering Group or PSG for short. I was the RN member of this group, and it occupied most of my time. Years later I was to draw on this experience when proposing further changes to this most effective organisation.

-----oOo-----

Social life in Washington seemed to be one long whirl and Antonia and I much enjoyed it. I was on the Diplomatic Blue List, which included all official supporting staff attached to Embassies and the like. The White List was limited to Ambassadors and diplomatic staff, and accredited Attachés. For them the social whirl was hectic. You were better off on the Blue List – typically two or three cocktail parties a week. There was a constant stream of official visitors to Washington, and any with a connection to naval communications or related matters were my responsibility. In addition, all one's contacts in the Pentagon and with other Commonwealth and NATO Navies (Canadian, Australian, French, and German etc) were "on my list" and were entertained regularly, and their hospitality reciprocated. Antonia and I entertained a lot, usually by way of cocktail parties. The Americans had an excellent custom which everyone followed, of always providing a cold buffet at the end of a cocktail party, which avoided the need to find food at home on return – very civilised! Before we left for America Antonia had made enquiries of the wife of one of my colleagues already in Washington – what clothes should she bring? The reply was short but accurate, 'Six cocktail dresses and an overall.'

Being on the Blue List had one enormous advantage, shared of course with the White List. TAX FREE! This applied to cars and the like, but more especially to alcohol in all its forms. This was available *by the case* from the Embassy, and made our own entertaining nearly painless. I found a small room in our basement with a lockable door, and it became our booze store. I remember once when checking what we needed for our next party, thinking 'Never again are you likely to say to yourself – only half a case of gin left – we need another one.' What made entertaining completely painless were the arrangements available to support us. Providing each event was cleared as official entertainment we got generous "entertainment allowances" based on the size of the party. In addition, much of the food for the obligatory buffets could be ordered from the Embassy kitchens, such as cooked hams, cold chickens, cold salmon (whole) and the like, at prices which clearly were only the direct costs. It made a lot of sense, as the British Government got a great deal of official hosting done for little outlay, far less than formally arranged events since all the organisation and personal effort were free.

There were several excellent waiters who, for a very reasonable hourly wage, could be engaged for evening parties. We used a splendid man known as "James" who worked at the Canadian Embassy by day, but was usually available in the evening. He knew his job backwards. The first time he came I was getting anxious. It was only half an hour before the guests were due and there was no sign of him. A minute later he arrived at the door, immaculately dressed in a black bow tie with a sack of crushed ice on his shoulder – 'In case we hadn't thought of it,' (we hadn't). He asked where the food was, and the booze and the glasses, what we liked to drink, and how many were coming. I could go and finish dressing – he would look after everything. He did. Half an hour later the guests arrived and all was ready. I discovered that he knew what drinks each guest preferred, providing he knew them already. By the end of the party he had done most of the clearing and washing up.

-----oOo-----

Another great feature of life in America was the ability to use the USN's facilities. This stemmed from sensible reciprocity – what we provided the USN with in the UK they provided for us in the USA. It meant that we could use the US Navy Commissariat or supermarket in nearby Virginia, much cheaper than commercial equivalents. More important in many ways was the availability of US Navy medical and dental facilities for free. This was of inestimable value during the summer of 1964, when our third child (christened John but always known by his family name Johnny) was born in Bethesda Naval Hospital – (but only just, after I drove Antonia there in an early morning race against the clock!). A few weeks later Johnny was christened in Washington Cathedral, a short distance away and where we went to church. One of his godfathers was a USN commander, who was in the same seminar as myself at the Staff College, and who had on completion moved with his wife and family to Virginia, to join the Pentagon. Antonia and I had become very friendly with Jim and Doris, they also subsequently saw much of us in the UK, and the two boys visited them as teenagers in the States.

Johnny's birth in America had longer term consequences. As he had been born in the States he would be entitled to an American passport, and be able at the age of twenty-one to claim US nationality – and also then to be in the unusual position of being able to become President – were that to be open to him. The other side of the coin was that we had to go through considerable bureaucratic measures to ensure that he was registered as a British citizen. Furthermore he had to be careful, during the vulnerable years of his youth, not to travel on an American passport to the USA or he might find himself drafted into the US Armed Forces.

There was rarely a dull moment. We discovered that far more people came to stay with us in Washington than in Hampshire, despite the fact that we had only a tiny guest room in the basement. Our nanny Josephine married an American sailor. The wedding was in the US Navy Church not far away. I gave her away, in the absence of her parents, and we held the reception in our little house. Josephine left, and we were fortunate to find a replacement, Iris, who had just left a Canadian family and was glad to join us. Our young family was growing up, and the following year Katherine, now a five year old, went to her first school and became a "little American". (She soon lost the accent on joining her English school on return the following year!)

In 1965 Winston Churchill died. He was a cult figure to many Americans, and the Embassy opened a Book of Remembrance in the Rotunda, a beautiful modern building overlooking Massachusetts Avenue. The place was empty apart from the table with the book, and a large vase of white chrysanthemums. It opened for four days from 10am to 8pm, and there was a respectful queue throughout. It was very impressive. All the British Staff of commander's rank or equivalent took it in turns to "attend" and answer questions for two hour stints, dressed in full uniform with swords and medals. One lady with a New England accent asked me if it was all right to write in the Remarks column that she apologised on behalf of America that the President (Lyndon Johnson) had decided not to attend Churchill's funeral in London, but send his Vice President instead. I thought very quickly and suggested that it would be more appropriate if she confined her remarks to her thoughts about Sir Winston himself. On the day of Churchill's funeral in London there was a large Service of Remembrance in Washington Cathedral, at which the Bishop of Liverpool was the preacher. All the same British officers who had attended in the Rotunda acted as ushers. It was a very moving occasion.

The final thing that made life in Washington so different to anything else that Antonia and I ever experienced were the long car trips away. I travelled a lot myself, mostly by air, to meetings and the like. But the car trips were very special. Provided one could plan to cover some useful duty occasion (with a written report on return) one could claim petrol allowance per mile, which meant they were largely travel free – we paid ourselves for hotels etc. Rather like the entertainment allowances, this benefited both sides. All of us on the BNS were able to go huge distances without ruinously expensive petrol costs, and the British Government was able to concentrate staff in Washington, where the main action was, but also cover many other aspects of the USA and get expert reports on them. Antonia and I made great use of these allowances, and we had three long trips away, and in doing so drove together, on Government funded petrol, through more than forty states of the Union. Not many Americans could say the same.

The first was in the autumn of 1964, when I visited one of the large radio transmitter stations providing the USN Polaris Force radio command link. It was VLF (very low frequency) radio, and every component was HUGE. There are very few such stations in the world – not enough room in that band of the radio spectrum to accommodate them. This station was in Maine, and with its vast aerial system occupied a whole island. The round trip took five days. We travelled up to New York State and New England, to the rock bound coastline of Maine. It was fascinating to see the variety of scenery in the States, and my only regret was that we could not spare the time to make a detour via Vermont, which by all accounts has magnificent autumn colours in its large forests at that time of year.

The second trip was down to New Orleans, which was celebrating the 150th Anniversary of the Battle of New Orleans, which was fought and won by General Andrew Jackson, who subsequently became President. In the process he beat the British Army sent out from England, killed its Commander, General Sir Edward Pakenham, and ended the war of 1812. The battle was in January 1815, and one of the reasons it and the whole war of 1812 hardly feature in British History is that it occurred in the same year as Waterloo, but Americans regard it as finally securing the independence of the States, and thus very important. The US Government had invited the British Government to participate in the various ceremonies, on the basis that the theme should be "the unbroken peace thereafter". Several Pakenhams attended as guests of the city, and HMS *Whirlwind*, a frigate, made a formal visit to the port and city. I was appointed by my Admiral in Washington as Liaison Officer for her visit, and Antonia and I drove down and stayed with the British Consul General and his wife. It was a fantastic week – grand dinners, parades, Mardi Gras balls, visits to the city's lovely garden district, and up the river to Baton Rouge. I look back on it all with great pleasure of the memories, but great sadness as to what has become of New Orleans since – ex Hurricane Katrina. It was being said at the time that the city should never have been built where it was, and that it was a disaster waiting to happen.

Our third trip was "the big one". I took a month's leave, Antonia's childhood nanny came out for an extended visit and took charge of the family and household while we away. We drove right across America to California, up the west coast to Vancouver, and back through the Canadian Rockies and the American Wild West. On the way we visited Yellowstone Park in Wyoming, via the "faces in the rock" at Mount Rushmore, and the "range" or prairie in Missouri. We spent a day to rest on the beach near Los Angeles, and went up the coast via Sequoia Park and visited friends in San Francisco. In order to claim the petrol allowances I visited the US Naval Postgraduate School at Monterey, and the second Polaris radio transmitter station in Oregon. It was all quite spectacular and unforgettable – not least the Rockies, where the clarity of the air and bright sunlight made it look as if you could lean out and touch the mountains across the valleys. We were away thirty days, and travelled on twenty them. We covered 9,000 miles in all, which meant that our statistics were an overall average of 300 miles per day, and 450 miles for each day on the move. It was the trip of a lifetime.

Next spring, in 1966, my time was up and I was relieved in my post. By this time our nanny Iris had left and her place had taken been by an "au pair", a charming American girl, Susan, whose family lived in near-by Maryland. She travelled back to England with us and stayed for a further three months. We took the family home by the liner *Queen Elizabeth*, plus our RH drive American "Rambler", an estate wagon bought tax free. We re-occupied our Hampshire home, not much the worse for wear after three years of being let, and with the money saved from the foreign posting installed central heating and a lot of fitted carpets, which we had discovered were now essential to our lives. America had been unforgettable.

8

Loud and Clear

Throughout my naval career the procedure for testing a voice radio circuit required one station to transmit to another the standard test message *'How do you hear me?'*. If all was well the reply would be *'Loud and clear'*. If not a description of what was wrong would be substituted – eg *'Weak and distorted'*. The problem, particularly during my early days as a communicator, was that it often *wasn't* loud and clear. An all too common feature of the reports of naval exercises (big affairs on a force scale) was scathing criticism of how badly communications had worked, and how this had degraded the value of the operation generally. There were many factors involved: old and unreliable equipment (particularly in the days before advances in electronics had provided the reliability we now take for granted); the need, decades before satellites, to rely on high frequency circuits for communications beyond horizon range (unreliable, noisy and full of interference); and the widening disparity between existing and replacement equipment when introduced (making inter-communication between old and new difficult or impossible). The resulting problems were that communication was slow or non-existent, the capacity of networks to pass information was severely reduced, and frequently messages were lost in transmission or received garbled. It infuriated everyone, not least my fellow communicators, who kept pressing our superiors to 'do something about it'. Dealing with these problems took years, many of us were involved, and I was in the thick of the process. Most of this chapter is about how improvements gradually came about. The subject is inevitably technical in nature, and I will try and summarise it down to essentials.

-----oOo-----

On promotion to commander in summer 1961 I was appointed to the Signal School, HMS *Mercury* as Training Commander (TC), and in charge of all instruction. However, the slow process of forming the new 'X' Section was reaching completion, and I was told that I was to be the first Commander (X) to get it up and running. My time as TC would therefore be limited to a few weeks only. The job was mostly general supervision, ensuring we got good overall results and time spent on courses was justified. The one particular thing I did, realising that I was probably the only person able to do so, was to re-introduce the Dagger C Course. With personal experience behind me I got approval in principle from above that it could be restarted for two officers a year, provided the course lasted only six months, and steps could be taken to ensure that only suitably qualified students would be selected. I travelled to Greenwich and met the Dean and heads of the Electrical Engineering, and Mathematics departments, and persuaded them that a suitable course syllabus could be covered in two academic terms. We planned to select students during their Long C Courses, looking carefully at their aptitudes and interest in "radio technical" and "radio theory", and adding to the selection process the Course Instructor Officers (Schoolies) who taught the latter. The scheme was approved and worked well. It provided a core of Daggers who over the years held the posts at which decisions on future equipment were decided, and was a major factor in the resulting improvements so badly needed.

That summer 'X' Section was formed at *Mercury* and I became Commander X. Its full name was 'User Requirements and Trials Section', an awful mouthful but accurate, and used as the full title to avoid treading on the delicate toes of those elsewhere who feared we were going to interfere in their work Our numbers were very small, apart from myself there were two officers in the 'Future Requirements' office, and three in 'Layouts and Trials' office. 'Future Requirements' work was based on complete Plans for the Future Fleet, drawn up at three year intervals ahead. These listed what equipment was fitted in

RN ships (with a summary of USN and NATO) showing how differences in the radio characteristics of old and new would inhibit inter-communication, and what might be done about it. The opportunities for this were limited in the case of new equipment already in the pipeline; but much more was possible when deciding the characteristics of totally new designs. This logical process replaced the old method of the Signal School commenting piecemeal on files sent down for scrutiny. The new methods took time to take effect across the Fleet, as most improvements had to wait until new generation equipment had been introduced. Even then there were more fundamental problems which had to be dealt with in other ways.

The 'Layouts and Trials' office drew up the arrangements (layouts) for the communications offices of new construction ships. To do this it was necessary to know what equipment would be fitted, which was based on the Plans referred to above. Arising from that you had to decide how each equipment would be sited in the office, and where such things as seats and desks would be placed. This seemingly obvious procedure led to an unexpected change. Once the layout had been approved we were in a strong position to argue what numbers were needed to operate the equipments, knowing whether they were to be manned continuously or occasionally. This led in due course to higher numbers of communicators than before, as there had never been a logical argument for how many were required. 'Layouts and Trials' also sent small teams to inspect ships' building, to ensure that details of layout and connections to aerials etc. met the specifications. They also carried out radio trials once ships were operational, to discover the degree of interference between simultaneous onboard transmissions, to judge how serious it was, and what might be done about it.

Previously, once a year there had been a 'Signal Progress Meeting' in London (at which the complaints I have referred to above were voiced). These were replaced by a 'Signal Progress Review' held at *Mercury* each summer, at which 'X' Section gave presentations on how new methods were being planned or introduced. We found to our pleasure that complaints from the audience were replaced with either approval or sensible suggestions. I much enjoyed my time as Commander 'X' and it was good to see that we were at last beginning to introduce the measures needed to deal with the problems so many of us had experienced.

My two years at HMS *Mercury* were up in summer 1963, and I spent the next three years in America. On return, my next appointment was at the Admiralty Surface Weapons Establishment (ASWE), the huge block of buildings on the top of Portsdown Hill overlooking over Portsmouth Harbour and the Solent. The great advantage was that it was only a few miles from home, which enabled me to continue to live there with Antonia and our young family, now rapidly growing up. It was summer 1966 and we had come back to a country which had under gone great changes since we had left some three years earlier. The "Swinging Sixties" had arrived, with the permissive society, the mini-skirt, long dresses for the evening, the Beatles and *Top of the Pops*, and an unmistakable sea change in life as a whole. The children settled into life in our large house and large garden, and went to nursery school; and finally to their preparatory schools, all local. Antonia became involved with daily school trips. Our lives were typical of friends of our own age.

ASWE had evolved through various changes during the Second World War when it had been an adjunct of the Signal School where new radio sets were invented, into a largely civilian run research establishment with much wider responsibilities, covering radar, weapons control equipment and communications. It was now headed by a Chief Scientist, with a naval captain as his assistant. The establishment had a very honourable history of research and development, in particular ships' radar in the

The Family ~ 1967

Our Hampshire home

war. It was also beginning to create the control systems for anti-aircraft missiles, and the large tactical computers and displays needed for aircraft direction and tactical control of a force of ships. On everyone's minds was the growing threat to surface ships of aircraft-delivered guided missiles, and the looming menace of sea-skimming missiles. The establishment handled many aspects of the still secret world of electronic warfare (which was beginning to affect all forms of naval electronics) and of course it retained responsibility for communications. Allocating resources of effort and money between these competing needs was the responsibility of the Chief Scientist.

During the 1950s and early 1960s the Communications Divisions of the Establishment had done sterling work on the design and introduction of new radio equipments, which were beginning to make great improvements to naval communications. The chief programme had been the introduction of transmitters amd receivers operating in the new UHF radio band, which provided tactical intership communication out to horizon range, and circuits for ship-aircraft communication to about 200 miles. This made communication within a force at sea and its supporting aircraft reliable, and as new associated cryptographic equipment became available such circuits were also secured from interception. In addition the establishment had invented and was introducing a revolutionary method of high frequency "wide-band working" which meant that HF circuits needed for long range ship/shore communication were far less prone to onboard interference with each other, and thus more reliable. Important and useful as this programme was, it nevertheless still relied on the basically unreliable medium of high frequency transmission via the ionosphere. It was not until it became possible for ships to use satellite communications that long range naval communications finally shed their underlying problems.

-----o0o-----

This was the longest appointment of my career, and although I recognised the logic of my posting I was not actually looking forward to the job, which was inevitably rather dry and technical. My post was entitled Communications Application Commander, 'Commander C' for short. There were several Application Commanders, and we headed the Applications Staff, some thirty naval officers who provided advice to the project staff (scientists and engineers) on the naval and user aspects of equipment under development. This covered such things as accessibility for use and maintenance, simplicity of controls and interconnections, sea trials of equipment under development, and very importantly, whether the equipment when finished would meet the requirements specified by the MOD. The latter was vital, as what had been specified initially by the sponsoring Naval Staff divisions (Signal Division in my case), and described in a long document known as a 'Staff Requirement' was inevitably broad in nature, and needed detailed interpretation during development. The scientists alone would not have been able to make the best choice, or indeed know that what they proposed was acceptable. The other responsibility of the Applications Staff was also to arrange and conduct sea trials of development models to ensure they worked properly before being committed to production. Most of the time both sides got on well, but occasionally there were difficulties, particularly if the Application Staff view was that what was proposed by the Project Staff was *not* satisfactory, and required further examination. This might well involve extra expense, or loss of time. I had direct access to the Signal Division and it was sometimes necessary to sort out what to do in such instances, in order to arrive at a mutually agreed solution.

Unfortunately, ASWE had something of a reputation in the MOD for not delivering its projects to time. There was an attitude amongst some of the scientists that they could not be held to account if development took much longer than listed in the Staff Requirement. 'Science is not like that,' I was told several times by the Head of Communications Projects. However, the Navy in London was getting tired of delays to development that were suddenly sprung on them, too late to do anything useful that might have cut corners earlier. Eventually during my time a systematic procedure was imposed by MOD, whereby the Application Staff monitored the progress of each project at six monthly intervals, with Project Leaders answering sets of questions at each stage. This caused understandable resentment, which was only partly allayed by a firm address to all scientists by the Captain of the Establishment, North Dalrymple-Hamilton. He pointed out that they existed to serve the Navy, that the life blood of the Establishment was the money made available from Staff Requirements for new equipment, delivery of which was subject to timetables which had been agreed with them. This was in the nature of a contract, and past failures had now made it necessary to introduce the new monitoring methods. It was not popular but it cleared the air.

----oOo-----

Despite these problems my relationships at Project level were good. In particular I worked very closely with the Satellite Communications Project Leader. This form of long distance radio communication was just coming into existence as a possibility for warships, as the powerful amplifiers needed for the very weak radio signals involved were developed. The Royal Navy was very fortunate in being able to use the American defence satellites, and eventually SATCOMS, as they were known, transformed long distance naval communications.

Early versions of SATCOMS were all introduced to take the place of long distance land-based High Frequency circuits, the only long distance radio band available until then, and very prone to unreliability and interference. Early SATCOM technology required large dishes, and development models for ships were of similar size and stabilised to compensate for ship motion. One or two trial models, or terminals as they were called, were sent to sea for operational evaluation, and necessarily mounted on ships' decks. The trials showed that they were far too large and heavy, which we already knew, but highlighted an even greater problem. Being at deck level the dish could only "see" the satellite if the ship's heading allowed it – if the ship altered course the satellite could be obscured (or "wooded", as it was termed) by masts and superstructure.

Effective operational communications require circuits to be continuously open, and it was judged impracticable to try and alter these methods to allow semi-continuous contact, or alternatively to require the ship to be manoeuvred to avoid wooding. The American Navy was having similar problems, and for a time it was not obvious how, or even if, the problem could be solved. The Project Leader and I discussed this frequently and at length. He asked – if the dish aerial could

93

be made small enough, and separated from the receiving and transmission equipment lower down, could it be positioned high enough on a ship's mast to provide an unbroken view of the sky? I advised not. This was the type of equipment which the Americans already had at sea, and they never succeeded in making SATCOMS a viable system with a "single headed" aerial; the prime position on top of the tallest mast would *always* be reserved for a radar or jammer, operationally more vital than a communications aerial. The solution that the Project Leader devised was to make the installation "twin-headed". This meant two identical terminals, each with its own associated receiving and transmitting equipment, the pair mounted as high as possible on the either side of the superstructure, so that at least one of them was in sight of the satellite all the time. Connection to the communications office and thus to teleprinters etc. was by way of long cables, and the best to use was selectable. Glanville Harris, the Project Leader (who very sadly died a few years later), was a brilliant scientist and engineer, and he designed and created the first workable ship-borne satellite communications installation. This was named SCOT (short for Satellite Communications Terminal), which was given super priority in production.

A further innovation was to fit every ship going into refit "For-But-Not-With" as it was termed – FBNW for short – so SCOT could be added to the communications suite later without needing full dockyard effort. This meant that as terminals were produced – and it took many years to provide enough for the entire fleet – they could be deployed to the ships needing them most. The Americans were most impressed, and there was a top level request for one terminal for their fleet flagship to be SCOT fitted – a rare example of the Brits getting there first! In a very few years time twin-headed installations became standard for all warships.

-----o0o-----

Eventually the measures described in this chapter, in particular the advent of satellites, plus the arrival of electronic techniques which provided modern equipment reliability, transformed naval communications. To those of us who could remember the bad old days it was a welcome change.

By the end of 1969 I reckoned that my chances of further promotion were very slim. The rigid system of promotion by seniority meant that I had only one more chance of selection and that was known as the "pool promotion" – all officers, of all specialisations, who would otherwise be passed over were considered as a single pool and the whole Admiralty Board decided which one should get it. I went and saw my appointer and arranged that in the event of me being passed over my next job would be Naval Attaché Stockholm. He advised me to wait in hope, but I insisted and my name was put down. The news would come on New Year's Eve, in the winter "half yearly" Promotion Signal.

On Friday 30 December at about 11 am I was on my way to my office when to my amazement Captain Rodney Bowden, my Assistant Director, came up to me, slapped me on the arm and said, 'Well done Bill, you're going to be a Captain!' I thought he was pulling my leg – surely the promotions weren't due out till the next day? But he was of course right; I had not realized that the signal would be issued *before* the weekend. Champagne was served immediately in the Captain's office. One of my colleagues had been in the same position as myself – in the circumstances he was extremely decent and congratulated me with the others. I jokingly said I wondered who would now go to Stockholm. 'You mean that job's vacant?' he asked. He excused himself, went straight up to London and got it himself.

Part Three

CAPTAIN R.N.

'It is upon the Navy,
under the Providence of God,
that the safety, honour and welfare
of this realm do chiefly attend.'

Preamble to the Articles of War.

(Inserted by order of King Charles II)

9

Planning for War

'Qui desiderat pacem, praeparat bellum'
Vegetius – 4th century AD
(He who desires peace should prepare for war)

Little did the savant who wrote those words in the dying days of Rome realize that they would so aptly summarise US and UK defence policy in the Cold War, some sixteen hundred years later. This was a matter I was deeply involved in for two years, and most of this chapter will be about it.

-----oOo-----

I was selected for promotion to Captain on 31st December 1969, which would take effect six months later. The week following the glad news I went to see the senior captain in MOD who handled the details of all captains' appointments, and somewhat to my surprise found myself discussing all my jobs in that rank for the next nine years. They were only "pencilled in" at this point, but with one or two minor changes represented the pattern of my career as a captain. It marked a great change for me. Apart from the obvious difference of higher rank, it meant the end of my time as a specialist communicator. For the previous twenty years, since qualifying in 1949 all my principal appointments had been to posts that required filling by (C) officers. Now, however, except for the post of Director of Signals (some five years later, which clearly had to be filled by an experienced communications specialist) all my other jobs were ones that could be filled by captains of any specialisation.

To my greater surprise I also learnt that my first appointment as a junior captain was to be to the Naval Plans Division, in the post of ADPP, or Assistant Director Plans (Polaris). I was told, and knew, nothing about the job, just that it was in 'Plans' – a division of MOD (Navy) of almost mythical reputation. I could hardly believe my ears. But it was true, and I would leave ASWE early and take up my new appointment in April as an acting captain for a few weeks. It would last until 1972.

-----oOo-----

The first week in my new appointment was even more astonishing. Nothing I had done previously had prepared me – in fact it would have been beyond the Navy to do so, as the job was unique. My predecessor explained it as much as he could in the first day of the turn-over when we were together, and I became acquainted with most of the rest by calls, visits, and indoctrinations in the following three days before he left and I was on my own. I was one of the four assistant directors in Plans, and responsible for naval policy for General War. Most importantly this included the policy for the Polaris Force, with the first submarines now operational (hence the job title). I would work to two "bosses" – my Director, who was a senior captain, as normal, but on matters of very high security where the strict procedures limited access to a named list from which he was excluded, I would work direct to one of the Assistant Chiefs of Naval Staff – a Rear Admiral – who was responsible to the Vice Chief of Naval Staff (VCNS) and the First Sea Lord. I later found this a somewhat awkward arrangement, as my Director not unnaturally objected to not being kept in the picture, but the security procedures were very specific

Apart from my own Director, I called on the Rear Admiral, the Vice Chief, the other Directors of the Naval Staff, and several others with whom I would be working in MOD. My predecessor took me over the street (Whitehall) to the Cabinet Office and introduced me to several people there who I would also be working with. I went for personal briefings to various highly secure places in the lower levels of MOD, where I was "indoctrinated" into the mysteries of high intelligence and similar matters which would be part of my professional life. Information on such subjects was limited to those who had a "need to know", and my name was added to the lists. Such matters were protected by a codeword, which had to appear on all documents dealing with them, and this was an added level of security classification to "Top Secret" which was followed by the codeword. I found at the end of the week I had collected about a dozen. Somewhat dazed, I started the next Monday, fully fledged and in the job.

-----o0o-----

Before I describe the job (or as much of it I am able to within security constraints), I must explain the way the Naval Staff worked, and the part in it played by the Naval Plans Division. The Naval Staff had been formed earlier in the century, to act as support to the Chief of Naval Staff – usually known as First Sea Lord, and the Vice Chief of Naval Staff (known as VCNS). These two officers were responsible for naval policy on all aspects of the Navy, and worked closely with the other Sea Lords, senior civil servants and Ministers, who with them formed the Admiralty Board. Decisions on *policy* having been made, with all considerations of money, men, availability of industrial resource etc. having been weighed carefully in the process, *implementation* of policy was the responsibility of others – for example, Controller of the Navy (Third Sea Lord) for provisions of new ships, weapons and equipment: Second Sea Lord for recruiting and training manpower: Fourth Sea Lord for repairs and maintenance, and supplies of ammunition and fuel, food etc. Operational command and control of the Fleet was the responsibility of the Commander in Chief Fleet, who was directed as necessary by VCNS. Various divisions of the Naval Staff dealt with various aspects of naval policy, but the central coordination of all policy from whatever quarter was the responsibility of the Naval Plans Division.

Coordination was effected by Plans by calling for papers from all relevant sources, extracting the essence and amalgamating it into highly condensed summary form, sending the results out to all, and calling meetings to consider them. The agreed papers were then further condensed into short papers for VCNS and 1SL (First Sea Lord). These were often discussed with them, and formed the basis for their briefs so they could discuss them at Board level, and policy decisions reached. Frequently it all had to be done in an extraordinarily short time frame; briefs were often called for by VCNS with only a week or so available to produce the answer. Plans had to work very fast, and so did those elsewhere who had to provide the input. There was no time to ring up and agree convenient dates for papers or meetings – at the most a telephoned warning that the process was under way. Meetings were announced and those summoned cleared their diaries and attended. They knew too well the penalty if not.

For their work, the staff of Plans were organised into four groups, some oddly named. The first, entitled 'Strategy', dealt with all current operational matters affecting the use of the Fleet, sufficiently important or political to be dealt with as policy – such as contingency plans for disasters or evacuations: a second dealt with all matters involving the Navy's commitments to alliances such as NATO or SEATO. The third, and in many people's eyes the most important, dealt with 'Size and Shape'; this handled all questions of what and how many ships would be needed in future years, what vessels they would supersede, how they would be armed, manned etc. It could equally have been named 'The Future Fleet'. The fourth, headed by me, was entitled 'General War', and was roughly split in two – policy for the use of the Polaris Force; and all other matters if peace ended and we found ourselves at war again. Being in Plans gave me a fascinating if hectic life. One got a totally new view of the Navy – I often thought of it as looking at everything through the wrong end of the telescope. Moreover, it provided an understanding of how the Navy was run that was completely missing from one's experience lower down, where one understood things happened "in London" that one took for granted and obeyed orders.

-----oOo-----

As far as my job was concerned, I will first cover that part of it which dealt with what would happen in the event of 'General War'. This term was something of a euphemism, as it meant all out war with the Soviet Union, to distinguish such a terrible event from something less than 'all out', referred to as 'Limited War', or hostilities with lesser countries. We were now, of course, in the Cold War, and much attention at high level (and vast amounts of money) in the US and the UK in particular, and NATO, were being applied to avoid the catastrophe of general war. Twenty-five years had passed since the end of the Second World War, and the period had been marked by a steady progression of events of increasing awfulness. The US monopoly of nuclear weapons had been ended with the Soviet Union acquiring them far earlier than expected. This led to John Foster Dulles' threat of 'massive retaliation' if the Soviets nuked America, but as the arms race built up, with both sides achieving something like nuclear parity this had become recognized as a policy of 'mutual assured destruction' (MAD). The concept of 'pre-emptive strike' entered the lexicon of war, and the possibility that the Soviet leaders might consider that they would be better off if they attempted to destroy all US missiles in a 'first strike' greatly occupied the minds of the Western leaders. It led to an even greater arms race, made a thousand times worse by the advent of thermo-nuclear weapons, and megaton bombs (Hiroshima has been destroyed by just one kiloton bomb). 'Overkill' and 'thinking about the unthinkable' joined the rest of the jargon. What broke this Gordian knot was the American development of the nuclear powered submarine, armed with nuclear weapons, which was named after its missile system POLARIS. The submarines could lurk deep and undetectable, and were thus invulnerable until ordered to fire. The Polaris submarines provided what was known as a 'second strike' capability, and it transformed defence policy in the Cold War.

The arrival of second strike weapons enabled a new defence policy to be adopted, based on *deterring* nuclear war, rather than *retaliation* if it happened. However, although a very welcome improvement, it didn't solve everything. Deterring nuclear attack left the problem of the Soviet Union's enormous conventional capability – in particular their massive armies and tank formations, and huge submarine force, which effectively placed Western Europe at their mercy. Nothing that the European nations of NATO, still recovering from the aftermath of the Second World War, could do would be effective against a determined Soviet campaign designed to bring Western Europe under Soviet control. The only protection available was that an attack would, under the terms of the North Atlantic Treaty, bring the USA into the war too. This was known as the 'American umbrella'. A new NATO Strategy was developed, based on deterring Soviet attack by methods known as 'Limited Response'. Any provocation or small scale attack would be matched by counter-measures of equivalent severity. Further provocation would attract further proportionate response, dubbed 'Escalation'. If the Soviets persisted it would be recognized that we were in a war crisis, and NATO would declare a 'Simple Alert', thus starting a 'Period of Tension'. Further measures would be taken – mobilisation of reserves in stages; commencement of convoys to reinforce Europe from America; the procedures for 'Transition to War' to put governments and nations on a war footing; and finally 'Reinforced Alert' – the placing of all nuclear forces at immediate notice. The intention was that this show of determination, coupled with the time taken for such events to occur, would cause the Soviet leaders to reconsider their actions, and allow consultations via the "hot lines" between capitals to bring about sensible solutions. Thank God it was never put to the test!

That part of my job which dealt with general war was mostly concerned with the previous paragraph – namely giving effect to NATO Strategy as far as the Navy was concerned. Much was already agreed, in particular the military aspects of what would occur, that is how NATO forces would be formed and used to provide Limited Response, and the detailed procedures to be followed. These included naval operations in the north Atlantic and Norwegian Sea, and the creation of the convoy system to reinforce Europe. Every two years there was a NATO 'paper exercise', involving all nations' Defence Ministries and Command HQs, but not operational forces, to test the procedures to be followed in a Period of Tension, through mobilisation and the NATO Alerts. If countdown to Armageddon can be so described – it worked well! What was still largely in the planning stage were the national procedures for Transition to War, to place the UK on a war footing, and this involved many government departments as well the MOD. As the Navy's representative I wrote the necessary naval inputs, cleared them with my superiors, and then attended meetings of various inter-departmental working groups in the Cabinet Office to hammer it all out. A surprising amount of things had to be agreed, not least the detailed measures that would be needed at each step. These were then added to the 'Government War Books' – huge tomes showing who would do what and when. There was a central version, with a carefully numbered summary of the various steps, and each government department had its own, with the supporting detail. It should be remembered that if such measures were ever required they would need to be effected rapidly, unlike in the Second World War where it all happened relatively slowly. The War Books provided the data that could be referred to without it all being worked out from scratch at the time.

Life in Plans was hectic, and often involved late hours, since Board papers required the next day that were agreed by the end of work had to be tidied up and committed to typing etc before leaving the office. In addition, the general workload was heavy, and one had to work late to get it all done on time. Fortunately, the recasting of Service pay had led to a fairly generous 'London living allowance', which meant that it was no longer ruinously expensive to rent suitable accommodation in town whilst maintaining one's home in the country. This was called 'weekend commuting', and it was much better than moving one's family up to London for two years. I was able to rent a very small flat in Dolphin Square, which served me well. Antonia looked after the house by the week, with all the children now at their schools by day. I got home for supper on Fridays, and left after supper on Sundays. Every summer we took the children abroad for a fortnight's holiday to France, or to Spain. Life was not ideal, but it was tolerable.

By far the most important part of my job involved the policy for the British Polaris Force. This was already operational, with several submarines in service and the rest to follow very soon. Much of the "modus operandi" of the Force had already been decided, and was the responsibility of others. My job was to deal with continuing matters of policy.

The 1963 Polaris Agreement covered the supply to the UK of the missiles, and their continued support, by the USA. The submarines and their nuclear propulsion systems, and the warheads, were UK designed and built. It was an underlying condition that the resulting second-strike deterrent system, although UK owned and operated, and under the political control of the UK at all times, was to be assigned to NATO in a war crisis. An important subscript was the understanding that in extreme national emergency the UK Polaris system would revert to UK sole national control. The conditions under which this might happen, the arrangements for reversion of control of the force to national command, and the resulting change of the targeting of the missiles to a national plan, were also understood, but never exercised. However, deciding the details continued for a considerable time.

American support for our Polaris Force was of crucial importance. We were dependent on them for the maintenance of the missiles, where we received a continuous flow of technical advice and updating modifications. Of equal importance, we were also privy to most of their high-level intelligence, much of which was secured by their satellite reconnaissance systems. Exchange of research information was also important, in particular underwater research which shed light on advances (or lack of them) in underwater detection methods which affected the invulnerability of the submarines. We had to be very careful to keep this all knowledge to ourselves; it was not ours to give away, and the agreements releasing it to us were specific. When the Conservative Government entered power in summer 1970 Ted Heath was keen to open up a dialogue with the French on nuclear submarine matters, and this led to much disagreement with the MOD. The Navy's top brass was adamant that nothing should be done that might jeopardize our excellent relationship with the USN.

The importance to the British Government of having its own independent second strike nuclear deterrent cannot be over-emphasized. Several sources of recent history have vividly described how, during the 1950s and early 1960s, the gradual realization of the terrible implications to the United Kingdom of all out nuclear war caused the British Government, both Ministers and top civil servants, an increasing degree of despondency, even despair. As well as the appalling casualties and physical damage, the UK would have been destroyed as a functioning economy. Moreover, the government was virtually in the hands of the US. Even during the later period, with the NATO strategy of deterrence, there was no absolute guarantee that if it came to a matter of risking America to save Europe, US nuclear power could be relied upon. However, by 1970 when I was in Whitehall, and with the UK Polaris Force deployed, I found none of this despondency, only a determination to ensure that Polaris would if ever required – and God forbid – deter the unthinkable.

It is necessary to explain why we were confident that our small force of submarines would, if it came to the crunch, actually deter nuclear attack against the UK by the mighty Soviet Union, a task similar to David and Goliath. To do this it was necessary for the Soviet leaders to reckon that such attack would result in 'unavoidable and unacceptable damage' to their country. The 'unavoidable' element of this was provided by the nature of the nuclear powered submarines. They could remain deep and undetectable (other than by chance encounter) for weeks if necessary. One was always at sea, sometimes two, and in a war crisis all three of the submarines in the operational cycle (the fourth reckoned to be in refit) would have been sailed and on station within range of their targets. Even though there might be an occasional encounter the Soviet leaders could not be certain that all of our boats were accounted for. The 'unacceptable' part was provided by the fact that the Soviet Union was a highly centralised country controlled from Moscow. The effective destruction of Moscow would have left their economy without a rudder, their military machine without higher direction, and the country at the mercy of the USA and China. It was judged that the threat of such damage to their capital was something that their leaders would not risk in order to '"nuke" the UK. The Polaris submarines each carried sixteen missiles with nuclear warheads, and if the whole force was targeted against Moscow, including any anti-ballistic missile defences, this would provide an effective deterrent. In fact, one submarine alone would have been sufficient.

On patrol the missiles were at short notice. Missile launch would be initiated by the 'firing signal' being transmitted via the radio broadcasts, known as the Command Chain, by order of the Commander-in-Chief Fleet in his bomb proof underground HQ at Northwood, acting on the instructions of the Prime Minister. This was known as 'nuclear release'. In the event that clear evidence showed that a first strike had 'taken out' the PM, Commander-in-Chief Fleet was authorised to act on his own and order the transmission of the firing signal. To prevent accidental firing, or the act of a maniac, each step leading to missile launch had to be agreed by two responsible men, each of whom had a personalised code to over-ride otherwise inhibiting controls. This was known as the 'two man rule'.

-----oOo-----

It had long been recognised that there was a serious flaw in the arrangements described above, as the Soviets could throttle nuclear release by attacking the large and vulnerable radio stations which provided the Command Chain, so preventing the firing signal from reaching the submarines. The availability to the Soviets of such pre-emptive attack thus, perversely, increased the dangers facing the UK during a confrontation. The solution was recognized; sealed envelopes to be opened on the loss of radio reception, with properly authorised orders for the submarine commander then to launch missiles. Such a scheme would, however, stretch the principle that Polaris was to be under positive control at all times. In addition it was considered that the absence of reception of the Command Chain, by itself, was not a sufficiently definite trigger. Harold Wilson, the PM during the late 1960s, refused to consider the matter, for fear of being pilloried by his own left wing if discovered and the subject had been dropped.

My predecessor had brought this impasse to my attention during our turnover – the file was still in the pending safe. However, in the summer of 1970 the Heath government won the election, and I decided to see if the matter could be reconsidered. As a communicator I realized that it was *not* necessary to rely solely on the apparent failure of the Command Chain to trigger a missile launch. In such circumstances the submarine captain could be ordered to listen out on all available radio signals, coming to shallow depth if necessary. It would be obvious from the disturbed state of the radio spectrum that a major nuclear exchange had occurred, and British and world wide radio broadcasts would be full of the news. If these conditions applied the captain could be authorised to open a sealed envelope and act on its orders. I was supported in my views by a friend of mine, a senior communicator in the MOD, also involved in nuclear release matters.

I drafted a short paper setting it all out and took it to my Rear Admiral to see what he thought. He immediately said he would put it to the First Sea Lord. Later that day I was summoned to his office and told to accompany him to see the great man. I shall never forget the occasion. Admiral Sir Peter Hill-Norton had recently taken office, and it was the first time we had met. He had a fearsome reputation. We came into his office, with its famous green baize table, and he waved us to sit down, me on his right. He came over with his papers, sat down, took his specs off, looked at me, and said loudly, 'I understand you wish to address me.' I swallowed hard, and launched into my subject. He listened in silence, and then said, 'I entirely agree. I will put this straight to No 10.' He instructed me what to do. The paper had to be reduced to two pages at the most. There was to be a short covering note, which should open with the words 'There is a matter of great national importance which has been left unattended by the previous administration.' ('Say that,' he said, 'and they will give you a licence to print money.') We withdrew, and in an hour the papers were back with 1SL.

I should say here in parenthesis that I realized that Peter Hill-Norton was testing me to see how I reacted under pressure. I clearly came through, because subsequently we got on very well, and he sometimes sent for me to brief him personally on points of detail on Polaris.

The proposal was put to Ted Heath, the new Prime Minister, the same day. It was greatly welcomed, and introduced immediately. Some echoes of what had been said in No 10 filtered back to me via my Rear Admiral, who presumably got them from the First Sea Lord himself. When the PM read the papers at his desk, with the Cabinet Secretary, Sir Burke Trend hovering at his elbow, he looked up, smiled, and said, 'This is fun. This is better than the Mersey Docks and Harbour Board.' Burke Trend himself said later, 'This is splendid. In a war crisis I will send for the Russian Ambassador and show him the papers, so there is no doubt in their minds.'

As I have said, one of the odd things about Plans was that once a matter of policy had been decided, it was implemented and became the responsibility of others. I never heard any more about sealed envelopes until I read during the last year or so that they were still alive and working well. I was also interested to read about the extreme reactions of various Prime Ministers when invited to decide what to put in them.

-----oOo-----

Almost unbelievably, although our Polaris Force was only just operational, the MOD had started to consider what should replace it when it reached it's "end of life" a decade or so later. It was not the life of the submarines or the warheads (which were British made) which were the problem, but the Polaris missiles themselves – which were American. It was known that the US was already planning the 'Trident' system as a replacement, and as we were dependent on them for the long-term maintenance of our missiles we had to reckon that their life was also affected. Planning and providing a replacement system would take many years. The Chiefs of Staff called for papers from all three Services, to put up what they could offer as a replacement as the UK national deterrent. It therefore fell to me to produce the drafts, which after much deliberation at higher level would be finalised and forwarded as the Navy's contribution. I well remember my feelings as I started work with a blank sheet of paper (no word processors then), writing the title and staring at it. I had of course discussed it all with my Rear Admiral beforehand, and the final version was submitted to the Chiefs of Staff, proposing that the Polaris Force should be replaced by a new generation of nuclear submarines, armed with 'Trident'.

The other two Services did the same. The Army wanted nothing to do with it, but proposed dotting land-based missile silos all over the Highlands of Scotland. The RAF were mad keen to get it; they had loathed losing the national deterrent to the Navy. They put up a paper proposing a new generation of bombers, with stand-off missiles, and a squadron of aircraft on airborne alert in a crisis. Before being considered by the Chiefs of Staff the papers were critiqued at meetings chaired by the Chief Scientific Adviser, Sir Herman Bondi. He was effusive in his praise for all of them. However it was really a "one horse race", and I was reminded of the jingle that had been current in America a decade earlier when Polaris was on the stocks. *'Put the deterrent out to sea, where the real estate is free, and the thing is far from me.'* The subject was considered by the Chiefs of Staff in closed session, and it was understood that it led to much wrangling. The Navy's paper was accepted, and the proposal was put to No 10 – all decisions concerning the national deterrent being the personal prerogative of the Prime Minister. It went through on the nod. It was many years before it was all acted on, but what should happen was not in question – just when.

I feel I should end this chapter with a personal tailpiece. For two years I was what is sometimes referred to as a "nuclear planner", and I made my contribution. Those of us who handled such matters were well aware of the terrible nature of the issues we dealt with. We had families, and moral principles, but we were dispassionate in our work, believing that the UK national deterrent was a force for the good which, if it ever came to the crunch, would deter nuclear attack on this country. Thank God the Cold War ended before our beliefs were tested.

10

Gibraltar

I had agreed with my appointer that my next job on leaving
Plans would be Captain of the Dockyard, Gibraltar. I badly
needed to become re-acquainted with the running Navy. Since
leaving the carriers in 1959 I had had very little contact with
ships, and there were whole new classes of destroyers and
frigates that I had hardly seen. There was no chance of sea
command, so the only way to meet my need was to become
one of the four captains who ran the four dockyards and
naval bases – Portsmouth, Plymouth, Rosyth and Gibraltar,
and who in doing so went onboard visiting ships, got to know
their captains, and generally became acquainted with how the
Navy ran at ship level. Gibraltar would also be very convenient
domestically.

Fleet visit to Gibraltar, 1973

113

As soon as my appointment was announced in the daily list I wrote to the captain already in post, to find a bit about the job, the official residence that went with it, and any tips about what to bring etc. I had known him since Dartmouth days and we had been together in Washington. To my surprise he was very off-beat about the job and Gibraltar in general. 'Rather an unhappy place,' was the tone of his message. I thought little more about it and reckoned that I would probably find it more amenable. When I left Plans a few weeks later I paid my farewell call on the First Sea Lord, Admiral Sir Michael Pollock. He had replaced Peter Hill-Norton who had moved up in the MOD hierarchy to become Chief of Defence Staff. Again to my surprise, after he had said some nice things about my time in Plans, he said he was afraid that Gibraltar was, 'not a happy place at the moment.' I didn't ask why, but started to wonder what I would find.

Antonia and I were looking forward to the Gibraltar posting. Our young family were now all boarding at their prep schools, and would fly out for the school holidays. We would not let the house in Hampshire, with the inevitable disruption this would cause, and it would provide a useful base if it ever became necessary for either of us ever to return for a spell. Our gardener, now resident in one of the cottages, would look after the place in our absence. However, as I had to take up post in the middle of the children's summer holidays I would go out alone and Antonia would join me later. I duly flew to Gibraltar in August 1972, and after a rapid turnover and calls I was in the job in a couple of days.

Gibraltar had been captured from the Spanish by Admiral Rooke in 1704. At the time it was an uninhabited rocky promontory, and the place was ceded to Britain in 1713 by the Treaty of Utrecht. The British recognised its commanding position at the gateway to the Mediterranean, and established a garrison there. It became the Fortress of Gibraltar. The Spanish tried several times to recapture it, but it was defended tenaciously. As the Empire grew, and with it the size and reach of the Royal Navy, Gibraltar became a naval harbour, with base facilities, and a small dockyard. Spain continued to contest its continued UK sovereignty, but the great sieges were a thing of the past. With the development of Malta as the Navy's main base in the Mediterranean, Gibraltar became a backwater. HM Ships en route for the Med hurried past for fear of being called in, far more interested in the fleshpots of Malta. This was the Gibraltar I had known in my previous appointments to ships; a great place for a Fleet Assembly, but not much else.

However, its importance had grown again in recent years. Malta was no longer a colony, and all HM Ships were now based in the UK. Gibraltar was our only overseas naval base, and within convenient distance. It gave sailors the chance of a "run ashore" abroad, without the complications of a foreign visit. With its generally good weather, and base facilities, it was a good place for ships' work-ups etc. There were, however, problems. Many of these had been caused by Spain closing the border in the late 1960s, as part of the continuing row over sovereignty. The civilian population was predominantly a middle class of shopkeepers, bank clerks and the like, dependent on cheap Spanish labour. No one had been prepared for border closure – amongst other things Gibraltar woke up to find there was no bread (no bakery). The Dockyard could not be operated effectively without the Spanish labour force and a hundred or so artisans had to be flown out from UK. Eventually it settled down, but Gibraltar was a changed place, with fresh food and much else previously available from Spain arriving by the daily ferry from Tangiers.

The other problems were caused by the fact that the Dockyard and Naval Harbour – its wharves, berthing crews, tugs etc. – were manned on a 'one watch' system, and only conveniently available Monday to Friday, 9.0 till 5.0. Outside those hours the civilian employees had to be paid overtime and

MOD instructions were to keep overtime to a minimum as an economy measure. Gibraltar had started to get a reputation for not serving the Fleet well enough. Warships arriving late on a Friday often had to wait at anchor in the Bay before docking alongside on Monday morning. Eventually C-in-C Fleet complained to MOD. This led to Flag Officer, Gibraltar – in charge of the lot – being replaced by a very determined Rear Admiral, Hugo Hollins, who set about "shaking things up". This included everyone having to work as required to serve visiting ships. This inevitably caused ruffled feathers. In addition he was given to sacking any officer he thought was not pulling his weight. He had already had his Flag Lieutenant and Staff Communications Officer, a charming but admittedly rather laid back fellow, replaced. And he had had continued rows with my predecessor – which explained his letter. This was the situation I found in my new job.

-----oOo-----

As Captain of the Dockyard (CD) I was in charge of all services at the wharf side and outboard, that is the berthing arrangements for ships and their alongside support, and for the moorings and navigational lights etc. I was also in charge of the tugs, lighters and similar craft and their crews, and the pilots. In these responsibilities I was excellently served by my very experienced Assistant Captain of the Dockyard (ACD), Lieutenant Commander Peter Whitlock, who had been a Commissioned Boatswain and before that a Chief Bosun's Mate. What he didn't know about wires, rigging, buoys and cables, and how dockyards actually worked, was not worth knowing. My further responsibilities as CD included the overall supervision of the work of the Dockyard Fire Service, which worked under the Chief Fire Officer, and of the Dockyard Police.

As well as CD, I was also QHM, or Queen's Harbour Master, an ancient office to which I was appointed by Royal Warrant, no less. In earlier years this would have been inscribed on vellum, but was now typed on MOD headed paper and signed by a civil servant. It provided a statement of what I had to do, and the powers the Warrant gave me. In many ways these were most imposing – I was required to supervise the 'use of the Admiralty Waters of Gibraltar, and secure their continued availability for safe navigation'. I was given the power of arrest of any vessel in Admiralty Waters that might endanger this. There was, as usual, a catch. I could only use my power if this advanced the aim. Of equal importance, although not stated, if I did *not* use the power of arrest when so required I would be in dereliction of duty. The Admiralty Waters comprised the Harbour, and approaches to it in the Bay, all in British territorial waters. I only used my powers of arrest once, and I describe this incident. below. In a similar way to CD, as QHM, I was excellently served by my Assistant Queen's Harbour Master (AQHM), Lieutenant Commander Bill Hurst, a Navigation specialist. He was responsible for the movements of all ships in the harbour, and produced a 'daily movements' list. This was important, as it was generally necessary to limit such movements to one at a time, to avoid accidents and collisions. He controlled the movements from his 'bridge' at the top of the main office block with an excellent view of everything, and he used the harbour radio net for detailed direction.

I should say here that this describes the workings of might be described as the Naval Port of Gibraltar. However, the base also comprised, very importantly, the Dockyard, which repaired and refitted ships, and had workshops and dry docks, and of course a large skilled work force, for the purpose. These were all under the direction of the General Manager (GM), who was also in charge of the Yard Services – the cranes, refuelling lines etc. In addition, Gibraltar was an important supply base for the Fleet – providing fuel, ammunition, stores and food – and this organisation was under the management of the Principal Supplies and Transport Officer (PSTO). As Heads of Departments, GM, PSTO and I all reported to F.O.Gibraltar.

-----oOo-----

Antonia came out in September having put the children back to school, and we settled into my official residence at No 2 Scud Hill. This was a very nice four bedroom house, with a large drawing room and dining room. It was an "upside down house", that is you came into the entrance hall and went upstairs to most of the accommodation. It had a little garden behind and up, and one day when planting tomatoes I found a Spanish cannon ball, over 200 years old – I brought it home as a memento. We soon found that Gibraltar provided a very full social life, with many cocktail parties and dinners. With the border closed the colony had to make its own recreation, rather than visit Spain as in the old days. The social round sometimes seemed almost frenetic, with everyone entertaining and reciprocating. Our social life was mostly with the British service officers and officials and their wives, and the few British residents of the Rock. We also saw many officers from the British ships which visited. There were also several charming Gibraltarians who were part of this circle.

Conditions in Gibraltar were difficult, particularly for the local population, and for the many British servicemen who had their families with them. Accommodation was by modern standards very poor and doing much about it almost impossible. There was an extreme shortage of space for new housing, since most of the territory was too steep, although a start was being made to create level building land by pushing out into the shallow water north of the Harbour. But even if there had been room to build there were virtually no building materials. With the border closed the colony had effectively become an island, and simple things like concrete and bricks that one takes for granted when delivered by lorry had to be imported very expensively by ship. What made matters worse for the Navy was that it had been necessary to draft in more sailors to man the various base facilities and communications required for the Rock's enhanced role. Although Chiefs and Petty Officers with families were reasonably housed many of the sailors' families were in post-war pre-fabs.

-----oOo-----

These conditions were at least partly responsible for an unlooked for temporary complication in my life. HMS *Rooke* was the naval barracks, which provided accommodation for all stationed naval personnel, and a holding unit for those in transit. It was in good modern buildings, but the sailors who had families were, as I have said, very poorly housed. These problems were exacerbated by the personalities of the Commanding Officer, a senior commander, and his wife. As his wife, she ran the Wives' Club, and instead of trying to calm the inevitable bad feelings about family accommodation, she fanned the flames, and in doing so enraged FO Gibraltar. It was really self defeating, as there was nothing that could have been done. The malaise affected *Rooke* as a whole, and the establishment started to become demoralised and inefficient. In these circumstances the C.O. failed to give a positive lead and took much the same line as his wife, with much the same effect on the Admiral. Eventually, after being warned, and a very poor 'Admiral's Inspection Report' (the place was in something of a mess) he too was sacked, and he and his wife left by air as soon as possible. It left *Rooke* without a C.O; to my horror the Admiral sent for me and said he wanted me to assume the position until the replacement C.O. arrived, as well as continuing as CD and QHM. I was thunderstruck, and wondered if it would be my turn next. I went and talked to the Admiral's Chief of Staff, Captain "Tubby" Fraser, a friendly and relaxed fellow with whom I got on very well. 'Don't worry Bill,' he said, 'you can't do much wrong. He can't sack you too.'

I decided to spend each morning in *Rooke*, and deal with such matters as office correspondence, Captain's Defaulters and Requestmen, and Captain's Rounds, and then go to my Dockyard office in the afternoon. 'Going onboard' the first morning I was already feeling somewhat fed up. There were four sailors working on the flower beds at the entrance. They glanced up but did not move. I was in uniform, and they should of course have sprung up and saluted. I didn't lose my temper, but I was certainly angry; the place was not only demoralised but clearly in a state of indiscipline as well. I parked my car at the edge of the parade ground and bellowed at the open office from where the routine was run. 'Quartermaster! There are four men at the main gate who failed to salute me – put them in the First Lieutenant's Report.' They duly got the appropriate minor punishment for such a misdemeanour. But of far more importance, as I heard later, my voice had echoed around the parade ground and well beyond. Everyone knew they had a new Captain. Later that day I "cleared lower deck" of officers, and addressed them around the Wardroom table. My speech was as you might expect – 'You have had a bad experience, but we must put it behind us. You all know how the Navy expects things to be run – get on and do it.' I ended with a phrase that I really meant, but again I heard later that it had sunk home. 'Finally, if there is something wrong, you tell me, and I'll tell the Admiral.'

I don't know that I actually had a considered strategy for how to deal with the situation. I know that at the time I remembered what I had learnt at Dartmouth running a house of sometimes difficult cadets as House Cadet Captain. I was certainly aware that one of the keys to success was to have the Chiefs and Petty Officers on my side, and was careful to visit their Mess for drinks etc. occasionally. If my policy for dealing with the confused and slightly demoralised state of the establishment could be summarised it would be – 'Be Friendly, Fair, and Firm.'

A quite unexpected remark finally told me I had succeeded. Some months later the Wardroom Mess had its Christmas Dance. As Commanding Officer I had a large corner of the anteroom set out for Antonia's and my guests, which included Jimmie Ritchie, the Surgeon Captain in charge of the Naval

Hospital and a personal friend. We were being welcomed by the Chief Steward, and all the Wardroom staff were bustling around serving drinks etc. 'Bill,' he said, 'what's happened? The atmosphere's quite different. You've changed the place!' In the spring the new Commanding Officer and his wife arrived, and he took over from me, and I returned to my normal duties.

---o0o---

The children flew out for their holidays, one month at Christmas and Easter, two for the summer. My residence was just big enough for all of us in comfort. In many ways it was an ideal place for them, not the large country garden we had at home, but everything almost on the doorstep, and plenty of other children of service families on holiday for friends. Their social life mirrored the grown-ups and they had many parties and attended local events such as the parades put on by the Army. In spring and summer there was both sea bathing and a pool. My barge was always available at the weekends, and in good weather we took it for picnics round to the other side of the Rock, to the sandy beaches there, or into the Bay for bathing. The two boys spent the occasional morning in the tugs (a privilege reserved for CD's children!) where they not only saw the tugs at work, but were thoroughly spoilt by the tug crews. Like all other people on the Rock, Antonia and I had spent a week or so in Morocco by ourselves, crossing in the *Mons Culpe* ferry. We visited Tangiers and Fez, and had found their markets and soukhs fascinating. Next holidays we went again and took the children as well. My parents, who were by now retired in Jersey, came out for a month or so in winter, and rented an excellent little tourist flat on the water's edge on the other side of the Rock.

One thing available in quantity, and within easy reach, was walking, I almost called it climbing. The "Mediterranean Steps", on the east face of the Rock, provided an excellent way to the top with its spectacular views. We took the children, and friends who were staying, up them many times. Another feature near the top was, of course the Apes, in their den overlooking the Bay, looked after by the Army, and with the long established legend that they would stay in Gibraltar as long as the British did. Then there were the caves, in particular St Michael's Cave, a huge underground cavern with stalactites and stalagmites, spectacularly illuminated by coloured back lighting. I should also mention the tunnels, although these were not open to the public. They were a labyrinth within the Rock, and it was said that there was a greater mileage of road underground in Gibraltar than above ground. Many of these tunnels were now used as ammunition stores, and others had been converted to large oil storage tanks. The tunnels were narrow and mostly unlit. They had been hand dug in the eighteenth and nineteenth centuries by navvies, and there had been many deaths from rock fall in the process. They were supposed to be haunted, and I must say that the few times I had to drive through them on duty and alone in my car they were eerie. The policemen refused to stand duty in them alone, and had to be stationed in pairs. I sympathised with them.

Life in Gibraltar was rarely dull. We had a continual stream of ships visiting, mostly British but Allied warships too. Many spent some of their work up in Gibraltar for a week or more; and during the two years I was there I saw nearly every HM ship in commission at least once. Ships visiting were always berthed alongside during their visits, and I met them at the harbour entrance in my barge, flying the ancient QHM's flag, and escorted them in. I would then go ashore near their berth, in time to be the first onboard up the gangway to welcome the Captain and First Lieutenant. All this had become something of a local tradition.

The most demanding of visits was a Fleet Assembly, not a frequent event, and only two occurred during my time. This would involve some twenty to thirty warships berthing in the harbour, with replenishment ships at anchor in the Bay. This usually meant "doubling up", that is two ships berthing alongside each other, and sometimes three at the same berth if they were smaller vessels like frigates. The berthing of so many ships involved carefully timed harbour movements to ensure those going alongside others arrived at vessels safely secured, with fenders out and ready for them. It was a carefully choreographed operation. Such events put my department on its mettle, to plan the movements carefully, and ensure tugs and berthing parties were in the right place at the right time, with wires, cranes and gangways available. Departure was equally complex as the planned movements had to ensure that vessels leaving their berths would have sufficient room in the harbour to make their way out safely, and in time to join the waiting formations in the Bay outside.

One visit was different from the others. A Turkish cruiser (Turkey being a member of NATO) made a fraternal allied visit, and was put alongside at Main Wharf, yards from the Admiral's office in the Tower. She was staying for four days. On the second day her captain requested to call on our Chief of Staff. He explained that one of his sailors had struck an officer. He had been court-martialled and found guilty, and sentenced to the only penalty allowed in the Turkish Naval Code for such a crime – hanging at the yard arm before the whole ship's company. Would we like that done on the side of the ship facing the harbour, or the side facing the wharf side and our offices? The Chief of Staff said he was very sorry but the death penalty had been abolished in the UK. Furthermore public executions were no longer allowed by law. The captain clicked his heels, said he entirely understood, and withdrew. Within half an hour we received a signal from the ship saying that it had an urgent need to go to sea for 'exercises'. It did so, and disappeared over the horizon into international waters. It returned the same day, presumably less one member of its crew.

-----oOo-----

There were other interesting incidents. One of these involved me arresting a ship. A large vessel arrived just off the harbour breakwater, flying the signals saying she was on fire and needed assistance. A nasty little plume of smoke was coming out from under her bridge. All our tugs were fitted as fire tenders, with pumps, hoses and foam apparatus and two were quickly despatched. The Chief Fire Officer and I were in the first away, and once alongside we scrambled up the chain ladders thrown over the side by the crew. We quickly discovered that the ship's engine room was on fire, its diesel fuel having ignited. Fortunately the crew had done the right thing and not only got the fire under control, but had sprayed the bulkhead aft of the engine room, on the other side of which were the diesel tanks – several hundred tons of ship's bunkers. It was very fortunate they had – if these tanks had gone up it would have been a major disaster. We also discovered to our relief that although shaped like an oiler her cargo was actually wheat. Meanwhile however she had no power, no engines, no rudder, and was unable even to let go her anchor. She was drifting and a danger to navigation as well as herself. It was a case for my powers of arrest. I radioed to the AQHM for the immediate typing of the necessary document. It was with us in quarter of an hour, I signed it, explained it all to the Captain of the ship – and attached it to the mast with sticking plaster. (The law required the document to be *nailed* to the mast, but it was steel.) Two tugs secured to the ship and she was brought under control. We sent for portable diesel generators, which supplied power to the capstan, and later electricity for accommodation etc. for the crew, and the ship was anchored. We had averted a disaster, but what the hell were we to do with ship, which was now ours?

This was settled remarkably quickly by the MOD. The ship was unable to help itself, so the owners agreed to treat it as a salvage matter. (Their insurance presumably paid.) In a week or so a huge ocean going tug arrived, and took it in tow to Naples where the cargo was landed. We heard no more, but the ship's anchor and cable had been slipped before departure. We raised it with divers and it joined our store of mooring gear.

Salvage was something that was never far from our minds. With the oceans full of ships, many of them hardly seaworthy, there were frequent calls for help, and often these resulted in the stricken vessel becoming a salvage case. It had become an established industry, and salvage tugs lurked at ports like vultures. One of our tugs was ocean going (the remainder being quite unsuited to heavy seas) and we sent it out to any calls for help in the area. We succeeded in salvaging one or two small vessels in nearby waters, which were brought into Gibraltar for repairs and settling of accounts, but most of the time the vultures got there first.

The laws and procedures of salvage were well established. The first rescue ship to get a line over to the stricken vessel, and thus able to tow her, had won the race. However, getting the stricken vessel to agree to accept help as "salvage" needed the captain to sign Lloyds Form A, and this was not always amenable. 'All we need is a tow,' was often the response when the form was presented. In the case of the RN salvage meant rich pickings; a lot for the captain, less for the officers and men, but *lots* for the MOD. The large book of Admiralty Instructions was explicit. Any ocean rescue provided potential for salvage, and all efforts should be made to get Form A signed. This led to a curious incident nearby on the Portuguese coast. A frigate returning to the UK from Gibraltar went to the aid of a small tanker, in danger of drifting onto the rocks, took her in tow, and got the Form A signed. The tow parted, and despite all efforts she went ashore. The frigate succeeded getting the crew off, losing one of its boats in the process. It was then discovered from the rescued captain that his ship was carrying highly toxic chemicals. This caused panic in MOD, as the tanker having been salvaged had become their responsibility, and cracks in the hull were starting to leak and contaminate the local waters. Gibraltar was told to send its ocean going tug to provide the necessary continuing presence of the salvor, so the frigate could proceed. We rapidly equipped our tug with food and appropriate stores, and I told AQHM to take command. They spent the next week or so happily anchored off a little nearby fishing village, as there was clearly nothing to be done about the tanker. The Chief Salvage Officer of the Royal Navy flew out to Lisbon and at great expense hired a car to drive him to the scene so he could clamber down the cliffs to see the vessel for himself. There was nothing to be done. Somehow the MOD divested itself of its responsibilities – they probably sold the ship for the value of its cargo, but we never heard if they made anything out of it, or perhaps lost on the deal. Within a few weeks the Admiralty Instructions for salvage and Form A had been completely re-written.

-----oOo-----

The final story I have of Gibraltar is an account of the felling of the sheerlegs. These large triangular structures had been invented at the turn of the century to enable the massive gun turrets of the "Dreadnoughts" to be lifted for servicing – many years before large floating cranes took their place. There was one at each of the naval bases, but the others had been felled already, and Gibraltar was the last one. They had been extremely difficult to deal with, and there been casualties at all of them. The Admiral put me in charge of safety. Balfour Beatty's "heavy gang" was engaged, and flew out for a fortnight, a splendid bunch of men. The danger was that if one of the three legs broke during the operation the whole contraption would fall and probably flail around. The gang inspected it all, made special arrangements for turning the huge screw which wound the centre leg forward, and tried to cushion the bottom of the front legs. The felling was done on a Sunday afternoon, the Dockyard was closed and the police searched the workshops. All Gibraltar watched, the privileged from the wharf side opposite, the more privileged from boats in the harbour, the others from roads and gardens all up the Rock. I was afloat in one of the tugs, and gave the signal to start. The screw started to turn, and for a minute or so nothing happened. The centre leg was beginning to buckle. At last the head pin turned, there was a vast jerk, and the screw forward continued. The sheerlegs were finally jutting

Ready ...

... on the way down ...

... SPLASH!

out over the water. I gave the signal to cut through the foot of the centre leg with acetylene burners, and we held our breath. After what seemed an age it parted with a loud bang, and the whole edifice shot forward into the water with a great splash. It had been hoped that its feet would jump out of their cupped supports, and the whole thing shoot forward and float. But it was stuck, and leaking fast. I had to think very rapidly. If it was left it would sink and block the berth. If we towed it away and it sank it might block the harbour. We towed it away, praying, and got it to the detached mole where it sank overnight. It was all made of very special steel, and a few weeks later it was raised and taken to the UK where it fetched a high price for scrap. Before it went I had piece cut off and mounted – "The Last of the Sheerlegs".

-----oOo-----

My time was up soon after, and we went home. Gibraltar had been a wonderful two years, despite its oddities and occasional frustrations. We had much enjoyed the social life, and seeing Morocco so easily. It had given the children some excellent holidays. And I felt completely in touch with the working Navy again. My next job beckoned.

11

Director of Naval Signals

'And what do you think, DNS?' It was Vice Admiral Sir Raymond Lygo speaking. He was Vice Chief of Naval Staff (VCNS) who, under the First Sea Lord, headed the Naval Staff in MOD. I was sitting at the table in his office with my fellow Directors, and he was considering a paper that would transform the way that naval signals policy was directed in future. On his instructions my colleagues and I had prepared and signed it, but it had been very difficult to meet everyone's point of view. and I had made it clear to the others that I would speak against some of the detail at the meeting. 'Well Sir,' I said, 'this scheme could be made to work, or I wouldn't have signed it. But I don't think it provides the best answer for the Navy.' I went on to explain why. There was a long pause and I held my breath. 'I agree with DNS,' he said, 'Have it re-written.'

-----oOo-----

It was late 1976, and I had been Director of Naval Signals (DNS) for a year or so. Even that was a close run thing. My planned career, agreed some five years earlier, had been that following my time in Gibraltar I would do the 'staff course for captains' at the Royal College of Defence Studies, and after that become DNS. I was looking forward to this and was much shocked to get a letter from my appointer towards the end of my job in Gibraltar saying that there had been a change of plan. I would instead, on return become the Controller of the Defence Communications Network (CDCN) in the rank of Commodore. I did not want this job, not least because it would mean someone else becoming DNS. I protested but it was made clear that it was that or nothing. With bad grace I agreed.

The Defence Communications Network (DCN) had recently been created as part of the rationalisation of defence matters generally, by amalgamating all three services strategic networks into one and scrapping what was not needed. The savings achieved had been enormous. The new post of Controller had been established at "one-star" level, to be held alternatively by an Air Commodore and a naval Commodore, to plan it all, to combine the bits into one system, and then control its operation. The first CDCN was an RN Commodore, Sydney Hack. He had done an excellent job of sorting it all out, and his successor, an Air Commodore, had got it operating well. It was now the Navy's turn to provide a Commodore to take the job on, but the Navy was claiming it had no suitable officer conveniently available to fill it. The RAF would have been delighted to do so, but the Rear Admiral in charge of the Defence Signals Staff thought the Navy should meet its commitments, and the Navy had to comply.

I was duly appointed, and drew my Uniform Allowance to fund the change of uniform to a Commodore's "broad stripe" in place of a Captain's "four stripes". It looked very odd at first. I should say here that at that time Commodore was a temporary rank, to which one was *appointed* but *not* promoted, and one reverted to Captain on completion of the appointment. It was an odd rank, and I used to say, 'The RAF call you "Sir" because they understand; the Army calls you "Commander" because they don't understand; and the Navy calls you "Bill" to make sure you understand.'

The main offices were at Medmenham, near Maidenhead, and there was an official residence, which I said I did not intend to occupy. (Antonia and I intended to continue to use our Hampshire home). There was a second set of offices in London, and this enabled me to again to take a small flat in Dolphin Square and claim London living allowance. I motored out to Medmenham most mornings – very easy against the incoming morning traffic. CDCN's staff was divided into two groups, the first concerned with planning and supervising the reorganisation that had created the DCN, the second to control the operation of the completed network. I found that the first group no longer had anything important to do – the work of reorganisation was over. The work of controlling the network was being very adequately done by the second group under a Group Captain. It no longer needed the Commodore to head the staff. I decided to wait a month or so until my Rear Admiral boss was relieved by an Air Vice Marshal, before putting it to him, and meanwhile made it my job to become personally acquainted with every radio station and comcen which we controlled.

This involved much travel, but I enjoyed it. My journeys close to hand took me to many radio stations and communications centres in the UK, very easy as I had a large official car and uniformed driver. Another trip took me to similar installations in Germany. The remainder were four overseas bases – Cyprus, Singapore, Hong Kong, and Gan in the Indian Ocean. If these visits were spread out to a normal leisurely schedule it would have occupied two or three weeks. But I was in a hurry, and to everyone's astonishment including mine, my swing around the world took me eight days, only stopping at each venue as long as needed to do the required visits, inspections and calls, and if necessary flying by night. My visit to Hong Kong, where I was very hospitably put up by the Commander of the Naval Barracks, was further enlivened by attending a Guest Night in the Mess within an hour of arrival, and going outside at nine o'clock to view an eclipse of the moon. On the way back I flew to Gan, a tropical atoll where the RAF had a large satellite communications set up. I arrived in the evening, and found myself accommodated in the C.O.'s lovely guest house (he was away) with its own private beach. I did my inspections the next day, and in the evening I had a swim, followed by a leisurely supper. I then embarked in the large RAF VC10 transport. As the senior passenger I was the last on board, and no sooner had I sat down than the captain of the aircraft came to ask my permission to take off. It was nine o'clock local time. We travelled direct to UK, with the sun, which meant putting our watches back. As a result we landed at Brize Norton as planned at 4.00 am. I was whisked through customs and passports, to find my faithful driver waiting for me. I knocked at the front door of my Hampshire home some three hours later, nicely in time for breakfast. It was winter, and a change from that idyllic beach.

Back at Medmenham, the day when the AVM visited us arrived, and I carefully left half an hour for our preliminary chat over coffee. After the usual pleasantries I said that, in my view, the reorganisation had been accomplished; control of the network could be handled by a Group Captain, and the set up didn't need a Commodore or the planning staff. He replied, 'Bill, I was going to tell you the same thing.' A Defence Review was in progress and he had to offer a number of officers' posts as "reductions". He could meet all his commitments by removing my post and the planners. I went and saw my appointer to warn him that I would be out of job in a few months' time. He nearly fell off his chair with astonishment. But he soon recovered his composure and said that was splendid, they were having difficulty finding a suitable replacement for me as prospective DNS, and I would go there as originally planned. It took some while for the changes to take effect, but in autumn 1975 I joined the MOD as Director of Naval Signals, thankfully wearing four stripes again. My planned career was back on track.

-----o0o-----

In addition to my normal duties as DNS there were two particular things that I intended to try and do during my time in post. The first had already been put to me before joining. Two of my fellow Directors had visited the Tactical School, where I was doing a short course to update me on Fleet matters, and explained that they had a message from VCNS saying that 'the Navy wanted its Communicators back' during my time as DNS. When they had explained, I was able to say that I was entirely in agreement. I had already thought I should try and achieve this. It was the pursuit of this goal that led to the scene I have described at the beginning of this chapter.

The major reorganisation of the Admiralty, War Office, and Air Ministry in the 1960s had abolished these as separate Ministries and moved them into a new Ministry of Defence as Departments of the MOD, with their own Boards. The new Central Staff had been formed by amalgamating several branches of the three single Services. One of the results was the Defence Signals Staff, of which DNS and his staff were the naval component. As a consequence they were *not* part of the Naval Staff. I had noticed this strange anomaly when in Plans some years earlier, as it meant that unless special measures were taken DNS's views were not taken into account when determining naval policy. As a result, future naval communications were beginning to be conceived in isolation from the new integrated systems which were increasingly the basis for all equipment.

DNS's responsibilities divided broadly in two. The first involved dealing with current matters of policy, very few of them complex or time consuming, such as revisions of flag ceremonial, changes to joint (ie tri-service) facilities or procedures, and matters involving all three services in 'transition to war' and similar scenarios. All these subjects had very little to do with the Naval Staff, and there was no argument for moving DNS and those of his staff which dealt with them. If they did concern the Navy deeply DNS had the right of direct access to VCNS if necessary.

The second set of responsibilities covered the supervision of the procurement of future equipment. Each element had to be "sponsored" via a Staff Requirement. In MOD the costed Staff Requirements had to be added to the schedules of future spending, within the allowed limits, and in competition with other Staff Requirements This involved much haggling. Progress through development also had to be carefully monitored, and kept in step with related ships' and weapons' programmes. All this work would be much better carried out from within the

Naval Staff, rather than at arm's length as part of the Defence Staff. It was this that had led VCNS to say 'the Navy wanted its Communicators back.'

This would mean partially dismantling the changes which had led to the establishing of the Central Staff. Top civil servants considered that gradually whittling away the individual Service Staffs, whilst strengthening the central element was the correct way ahead for the MOD. 'Giving the Navy its Communicators back' looked suspiciously like reversing the proper trend. VCNS had prepared the ground at his level, and it had been agreed in principle that he could propose changes that would leave the Defence Signals Staff effectively in place. We had to square this circle, and there was no simple solution.

The only way to enable DNS to continue to be the focus for future communications policy, but within the Naval Staff, was to rename him Chief Naval Signal Officer (CNSO) with the additional title of Deputy Director Operational Requirements, and move his office up to the Naval Staff floor. As CNSO, he would continue to have the right of direct access to VCNS, but on normal matters would work under the Director Operational Requirements. Those members of his staff who dealt with future communications matters would move up with him. To meet the need to leave the Defence Signal Staff basically unchanged CNSO would remain the naval member of the Defence Signal Board. His staff, other than those moving, would remain in place in their existing offices, with the same responsibilities.

On all these matters there was agreement between me and my co-directors. The difficulty between us was who would control those members of CNSO's staff who moved up with him. It was agreed that they would have normal lines of responsibility within their new divisions, except that on matters of signal policy they would work direct to CNSO. The problem lay in the all important "wiring diagram'" showing the lines of responsibility. All the lines to CNSO were "dotted", and it was made clear that these covered "coordination" not "control", and that the final word on such matters rested with the other directors. My argument rested on another part of my responsibilities as DNS, and I deal with this below.

As far as family life was concerned it was a similar existence to that which I had had in my days in Plans – weekend commuting. The differences were that I had a rather larger flat in Dolphin Square, one bedroom, with a small living room, and with all the children at boarding school Antonia was able to come up quite a lot, usually for events and theatres. We entertained a certain amount – my fellow directors and my bosses, and their wives. What made a lot of difference to me was that the job was not nearly so demanding as the one in Plans, and I was far less tired in the evenings and at weekends. We continued to give the children nice foreign holidays in the summer.

My personal life as DNS was different to that in Plans in many other ways. I was now of a seniority, and a position, to be on the lists of electronics manufacturers who aspired to sell their wares to the Navy. I visited all of them and was very interested to see their factories and naval equipment in various stages of production. They also entertained a lot, usually via their all important trade associations, and I went to many sumptuous dinners etc. As well as such high life, I also made it my business to visit every radio station and communications centres that provided long distance services for the RN; we were completely dependent on them to communicate with the Fleet, and although they were administered by local flag officers, operationally speaking DNS was very concerned to know that their staff were happy, that there was nothing starting to go wrong – and if so to put it right. I also found it much easier to deal with papers affecting these facilities and to discuss them with my bosses if I could picture the place and its staff. The other matter which took me away from London was DNS's responsibilities for "allied communications". It was this which caused my difficulty with "dotted lines" that I have alluded to above, and it also involved the second of the tasks I had set myself.

There is a marked difference between communications equipment and most other naval equipment. Put a gun in a ship and it will do its job. Put a radio set in a ship and it will only do its job if there are other radios elsewhere it can communicate with; these therefore have to be sufficiently similar, or "compatible", that inter-communication is possible. Providing for this with British equipment was the job of DNS and his crew, and how this was achieved is covered in earlier pages. It was becoming more difficult as communications became more complex.

This general problem was made far worse when it came to providing the communications for allied operations, such as those called for by NATO, where naval task groups of mixed nationality were part of the concept of operations. The difficulties had been recognised when NATO was formed, and one of its Agencies was specifically charged with the problem; in fact one of my ex-officio tasks as DNS was to head this Agency, with a small secretarial staff in London, and working direct to the Communication Staffs at NATO HQ in Brussels. The Allied Naval Communications Agency, or ANCA as it was called, produced plans for naval operations, and standardisation agreements for future equipment, and its Committee, composed of all NATO Navies' Directors of Naval Communications, met twice a year to take decisions. This was all splendid, but it was a carrot not a stick, as with so much else in NATO. It served the needs of the middle sized navies of the UK, France, Holland and Germany but not an alliance that included the USA at one extreme and Greece and Turkey at the other.

The problem for the RN lay with the increasing technical disparity with the USN, exacerbated by the speed at which the USN designed, produced and fitted equipment. This had been foreseen and was being tackled via the NAVCOMS Organisation which I had been part of in Washington. As DNS I was now the British Member of the Navcoms Board and attended meetings regularly. I became critical that the Board was being too bland in its reports to the Heads of Service. 'Yes we have problems, but we have plans for dealing with them.' This resulted in a thankful "tick" and the report being consigned to the archives. The danger was twofold. First, by the time that a problem had become operationally apparent it would be too late to do much about it in the short term. Second, what money and effort *was* available to devote to international inter-communication could be much better spent on essentials rather than spread ineffectively across the board.

I went and saw my Rear Admiral boss who dealt with future equipment matters, and agreed with him that what was needed was a realistic report from the Board which said just that. This should trigger a meeting of the NAVCOMS Super Board. This was allowed for in the scheme, but in view of the bland reports had never met. I wrote a paper for NAVCOMS entitled 'Communications between Navies of different Nationalities', subtitled 'A Methodology', and of course the subtitle stuck! It described the problems and how they had arisen, and then went on to propose that there should be three plans, one covering the present; one five years ahead and based on new equipment already in the pipeline (and thus unalterable); and one ten years ahead, covering new equipment still under consideration. The content of these plans should be the types and nationalities of ships, the equipment they carried; and the communications circuits that such equipment would provide. This approach would in my view go a long way to provide a proper evaluation of where we were all going. "Methodology" went down well, and I was surprised to be told by the First Sea Lord, Admiral Sir Edward Ashmore – and himself an ex-communicator – when calling on him for something quite different, that during his recent regular meeting with the American Chief of Naval Operations, he had been told that it had been much appreciated.

A few months later we had the next NAVCOMS Board Meeting. I was pleased to find that there was general agreement that our report should be realistic. As a result, when our report reached our Heads of Service they agreed by exchange of letters that the Board's report should be referred to the Super Board, which should be convened for the purpose.

The Super Board met a few weeks later to allow a Working Group, which had been set up to apply 'Methodology', to produce a report. The Super Board Meeting was in Ottawa, very impressive, four Admirals headed by an American Vice Admiral (my Rear Admiral boss represented the RN), all the Directors of Naval Communications (ie the Board) in attendance, and a large contingent of supporting staff. After the usual opening remarks and pleasantries, it got down to business. The Chairman called on the USN staff officer who had led the Working Group to make his report. His opening remarks included the sentence 'Methodology showed us what doors to open and in every cupboard we found a can of worms.'

The meeting was surprisingly short and businesslike and the Super Board's report to Heads of Service was simple. It concluded that the technical problems of increasing incompatibility between the USN and the other Navies meant that although inter-communication was satisfactory at the present, it would inevitably fall during the next ten years to the point where it would no longer be practicable to use integrated tactical formations as in the past. This would mean that USN naval formations would then have to operate separately from those of other nations. The limited resources available should be directed towards ensuring that the fewer circuits needed for such a concept of operations were given priority. The Super Board made a further and far-reaching proposal. It noted that the increasing use of computers in navies and support services such as intelligence made it vital that they and their software and data links were compatible. It proposed that the NAVCOMS Organisation, which covered communications, should have a parallel arm covering computers, also reporting to the Super

Board. The report was accepted and given immediate effect. I had completed the second of my main tasks. These bureaucratic events caused hardly a ripple outside ministries at the time, but they transformed the way that allied naval communications were planned during the Cold War, and probably beyond.

-----o0o-----

I still have to deal with the issue of "dotted lines" and what I said to VCNS in my little speech. I pointed out that, unlike the other specialisations, Communications had to provide the Navy with the ability to talk to other navies. This involved much international negotiation, including the reaching of understandings based on commitments with the Directors of Signals of other Navies, all of whom controlled their own signal policy. In his new "hat" CNSO would be greatly weakened if he was known only to "coordinate" policy. The paper was revised to everyone's satisfaction, and – to everyone's relief – agreed at MOD top level.

The new organisation was announced to the Navy in a long Admiralty Fleet Order, and I spoke to all my staff, explaining why it had become necessary and saying that it had my full support. A week or so later the new title of Chief Naval Signal Officer was introduced, and I became the last DNS and first CNSO. The actual changes in offices, and the new titles and duties for my staff, were delayed until I left a few weeks later, my place and new title being taken by my Deputy.

I much enjoyed my two years as DNS, which seemed a fitting finale for my long career as a communications specialist. Meanwhile, my last appointment as Captain had been decided. I was to become the Director of the Royal Naval Staff College, Greenwich – a mere boat trip down river.

A trip down river, 1977

12

Greenwich

'Oh yes! Power is a great aphrodisiac', said my guest in his broad Welsh accent, sipping his wine and seemingly very pleased with himself. He was Clive Jenkins, Secretary General of a white collar Trade Union, and a national figure. We were in the Painted Hall, and after dinner he would talk to the Staff Course in the Mess Anteroom. The Staff College had these soirées twice a term, usually for left wing or controversial speakers. The good dinner beforehand helped loosen tongues.

We all listened to him. He explained that his post as Secretary General was a life appointment so he couldn't be displaced. He told us what he did with his "powah" – or at least most of it. The Staff Course were restrained in their questions. At the end I carefully thanked him for his "illuminating" lecture. We ushered him into his chauffeur driven limousine and he drove off.

-----oOo-----

I hosted most of the Staff Course lecturers and speakers in this way, mostly of course for lunch following their address. Clearly they all welcomed the experience of being entertained in the Painted Hall. In fact I had discovered this much earlier during my Dagger C Course in 1952. One could invite anyone, however grand, and they all accepted if it meant dining in the Painted Hall.

My father and I had attended Greenwich several times over the years. He had done his Dagger G course there in the 1920s, the Staff Course in the 1930s and the War Course in the early 1950s. I had done my Dagger C Course there in the mid 1950s; and my appointment as Director of the Naval Staff College was my last job in the Navy.

I had thought that running the Staff College might be a rather dull administrative job, supervising officer training, with none of the intellectual challenges and heady office politics of the MOD. I was right about the latter, but wrong about it being dull. I found it stimulating and extremely busy, and certainly "different". There were also one or two very nice perks that went with it. Not many people can point to one of the buildings in Canaletto's famous painting and say, 'That was my bedroom window'.

-----o0o----

Greenwich (College, Palace, Hospital – call it what you will) was a beautiful place, with a long and tangled history. Its Royal connections can be traced back to William the Conqueror and before, and in the 15th century King Henry VI completed the Palace of Placentia, which was home to all the Tudor monarchs. The beautiful Queen's House, now the centre building of the National Maritime Museum, was built in the early 1600s by Inigo Jones to the order of James I for his wife Queen Anne, who found the old palace too damp. This was the first classical building in England and considered by many to be the model for the English Georgian style. The old palace fell into disrepair during the civil war. Following the Restoration Charles II started to build a replacement but ran out of money. Greenwich Observatory was however built on the foundations of a Royal watchtower on the bluff over looking the river. It was not until Sir Christopher Wren was commissioned by William and Mary to complete it all that it looked as it does today, The cartoon on page 136 may help.

The Queen's House became the central focus for Wren's design, and what remained of the brick rubble of the old palace was pushed into the Thames to allow the Queen Caroline Building, architecturally similar to the already completed King Charles Building, to be constructed on the opposite side of the Grand Square between them. Behind these two river front

River Front, Greenwich. Staff College in background.

buildings were the King William and Queen Mary Buildings
(domed in the cartoon) housing the Banqueting Room known as
the Painted Hall, and the Chapel Royal, now Greenwich Chapel.
The "usual offices" on the same sumptuous scale were provided
behind. However, the Royals found Greenwich an unpleasant
place to live – foggy and dank, and far too big for their tastes.
But what to do with such an expensive white elephant?

A fortunate solution was at hand. The Anglo-Dutch
Naval Wars had left many crippled and indigent old tars. The
Navy was given Greenwich as a Hospital for them, the naval
equivalent of Chelsea. What the pensioners made of the Painted
Hall as their dining room we don't know, but by many accounts
the place was a sink of iniquity. This situation lasted nearly two
hundred years, until the end of the nineteenth century when
the pensioners were given incomes rather then lodgings, and

the place lacked a role again. Fortunately, one was available. The Navy was converting from sail to steam and wood to steel, and from muzzle loaders to the big gun. The "Dreadnoughts" revolutionised naval warfare. All this needed much specialised education, and Greenwich became the Royal Naval College. Science, Mathematics, Engineering, Ballistics, Metallurgy etc. were all taught, and for decades Greenwich College was reckoned to be the maritime "state of the art". There were many departments, and these changed over the years as the need for new skills arose. It became a major site for officer training, and the Staff College was one of the subsidiary departments of the Main College, which was under the command of the Admiral President. This was still broadly the position in 1977 when I joined.

-----oOo----

The Staff College occupied most of the Queen Caroline building. The maximum course size was about seventy, but this varied. The norm was about forty-five RN students and fifteen others. The latter were a mix of Army and RAF, Commonwealth Navies, and foreign navies. It was noticeable that the students from foreign navies were often of exceptional ability, as these were coveted postings and strictly rationed. Their navies only sent their best and many went on to head their service. Our own students were not all so outstanding, but many of those that passed through during my time later achieved high rank.

The RN Staff Course had three objectives; namely to prepare students for a position as – (a) desk officer in MOD; (b) staff officer to a Flag Officer; (c) for command at sea. The first two were obvious, but I had difficulty in seeing what particular instruction was relevant to the third. Unlike the Army, where the skills learnt at Camberley were essential for middle and higher rank, the Navy's training for sea command was provided by the Tactical School, and the thorough "work-ups" that ships went through before joining the Fleet. The course curriculum covered logical thinking; style and conventions of Service writing; a general understanding of how the Army and Air Force were structured and organised; a good understanding of NATO Strategy and procedures, and the organisation of Flag Officers' staffs and MOD.

One of the many paradoxes of Greenwich was the near impossibility of getting any alterations done. (The Royal Fine Arts Commission and the Planning Regulations for Grade 1 Buildings looked after that.) Despite its recognised function the College had taken years to get approval to build a proper tiered lecture hall, named Briggs Hall after the Director who finally succeeded, but this was now available. With this in place accommodation for teaching and administration was good. Most instruction was done in syndicates, groups of about eight – carefully mixed. Big "schemes" were done as a team, and presented and then critiqued by the whole course. There was rarely a dull moment – if there was it was a mistake!

Much of the Course was spent "broadening the mind" on matters that, as middle rank officers, they would probably not have known much about. In my opening address to students – other than the obvious remarks like congratulating them on being selected, the importance of staff training etc., I told them that they were about to experience several months of being put through a "mental gymnasium". There was a most impressive list of lecturers and speakers, from Universities, Industry, the Civil Service, and Politics. Most top officers in the Navy addressed the Course. There were two lengthy "field trips" away – to Brussels, where we visited the European Commission, and NATO Headquarters, and we also had an excellent tour of the battle field of Waterloo. The other was a hike around Fleet Headquarters, the Polaris Base at Faslane, and a Dockyard. There was also an important fortnight in each Course when the students of all three Service Staff Courses attended a combined period at Camberley. There were also field trips to an RAF air station, and the Army on manoeuvres on Salisbury Plain.

Most evenings were occupied one way or another – we worked the Staff Course hard during the normal working day, and into the "dog watches" and beyond, with lectures, dinners and evening soireés with speakers There was also much entertaining. As Director, I invited every student (and wife) to at least one party in my official residence. There were frequent Mess Dinners in the Painted Hall, with some very grand occasions such as Trafalgar Night – with eminent speakers. And there were the magnificent summer and Christmas Balls. The interest came from the occasions themselves, of course, but more particularly the top-notch people that came to address the Course, who I met and hosted. They were all well known in their fields, and meeting them widened one's view of the world.

In addition to the students, of course, there were their instructors, known as the Directing Staff. There were a dozen of these, mostly British, with Commonwealth and USN colleagues, and an administrative staff of four (the continual arranging of lecturers to visit, and Course trips away etc., made for a heavy administrative load). These were all headed by my Deputy Director, a junior Captain. Like the Course, the Directing Staff never had a dull moment, setting, correcting and then evaluating students' work, which reached me in final draft form, for my "imprimatur". The most important bit was translating it all into the students' "confidential reports", which would go into their personal files in the MOD, and could make a lot of difference to their promotion prospects. A good report from the Staff College would not automatically lead to promotion, but it could tip the balance. A bad report could have the opposite effect.

-----oOo-----

My official residence was at the end of the Queen Caroline Building, overlooking the Thames. It was on two floors, the third floor being separate accommodation for senior staff at Greenwich. The other residence next door was that of the Dean of the College. Across the Grand Square the main residence on the river front was that of the Admiral President, and alongside that the Captain of the College. They were all magnificent houses, with long histories. Hardy, of Nelsonic fame, was Captain in his day and Nelson used to stay with him. The place was rife with stories and rumours – one of the antique windows in my bedroom had a diamond scratch which was supposed to have been made by Lady Hamilton, but it was impossible to verify this.

Inevitably, of course there were innumerable ghost stories. Some were clearly wrong – my residence was said to be haunted by Anne Boleyn bemoaning her departure for the Tower, but the steps she left from had been many metres inland; my residence was built on the brick rubble Wren had had pushed into the river. Some of the better supported stories may have had more substance. One of the staircases in the Staff College had several reported sightings of wraiths, and at least one very strange photograph. In my residence one of our bedrooms had a "nasty feel" to it and in the past children were said to have awoken screaming. It certainly did feel a bit different to the other bedrooms, and we did not use it much for guests or our own children.

Three times while I was alone in the evening I had close encounters with ghosts, and my experiences changed my attitude. The first was when I was in the bedroom upstairs, and I heard the unmistakable sound of tinkling tea cups down below in the drawing room. With the hair rising on my neck I went down to find everything normal and quiet. I went up again, and once again the tea cups started to rattle. I finally worked it out. There was a large and beautiful candelabra in the drawing room below, and my weight on the beams above moved the ceiling very slightly. The second occasion was when I was working late in my study. I heard the clatter of dishes and plates in the kitchen, to my surprise as I thought that my cook had left some time ago. I called out, but no reply. It happened again and I found it unpleasantly odd. Just before going up to bed I decided to have another good look round. While I was in the kitchen, the same sound occurred. It had come from the fridge. I found that this had switched itself on, which had rocked it and two badly stacked dishes had rattled.

The third visitation really did fill me with dread, and it took longer to discover what it was. It was one evening during a storm. There had been power failures and the lights were dim. I was alone in the drawing room when a quiet moaning started. It rose and fell like someone in agony. It was so low in pitch you couldn't tell where it was coming from – it filled the room. I at last reckoned it was somewhat stronger near the fireplace, where there was a large electric fire in front of the blanked-off old grate. Behind, I discovered a small six inch tear in the blanking sheet, which was made of thick wallpaper. The high wind in the flue was causing this crack to vibrate, and the chimney to resonate like a low pitched organ pipe. Once understood, terror banished! I got a large piece of sticking plaster and turned the organ recital off.

-----oOo-----

Although I spent most evenings on my own, Antonia was able to join me a lot. Our children's education had reached the stage when her presence in our Hampshire home was not required all the time. The two boys were boarding at public school, and Katherine was a day pupil at sixth form college and could stay with friends from time to time. By careful planning Antonia was able to act as hostess at all our dinner and cocktail parties in the residence, and to accompany me for most of the reciprocal invitations. This was made much easier because I had a staff of two, a cook, and a steward to wait. We gave large parties for the big Summer and Christmas Balls, and had many of our friends to stay the night for them. Other friends visited us too, some from far afield. One couple on holiday from America – he was Johnny's godfather who we first knew in Washington – stayed a few days. He was a "history buff" and fascinated to find himself only yards from the Maritime Museum. They distinguished themselves by going to Scotland via France. I had carefully directed them via the South Circular Road (years before the M25). We got a letter from Scotland some two weeks later to say that on the way they had they had noticed the signs for Canterbury and had decided to detour to look at the Cathedral. Whilst there they noticed the signs for the ferries for France, and decided to do that too.

Much of the interest at Greenwich came from the incidentals. It certainly taught me to think on my feet. One of my duties was to host all the important speakers, who lectured the Course on most mornings, last session before lunch. After preliminary coffee I would escort them into Briggs Hall and introduce them. I would then sit and listen carefully; I had to make notes as they talked, decide what to say in relevant comments at the end, after questions, and then thank them. As one had to mount the stage for the latter, without notes in one's hand to make it look spontaneous, it was vital not to have a temporary mental blockage. The worst thing that could happen – and it did happen to me once – was to forget the speaker's name!

I was already used to getting up in front of people – my period as instructor at the Signal School had seen to that. But I shall never forget the first time I made the after-dinner speech at a Guest Night in the Painted Hall, speaking from the Upper Hall and looking down into the long vaulted Lower Hall. It was vast, and one felt like a small pea in a very large and beautiful pod. In fact, that was not the most daunting place to speak – Alanbrooke Hall at the Army Staff College, Camberley – which we visited for combined staff training – was universally recognised as such. Its highly tiered seats meant that wherever the speaker's eyes might wander he was always looking at another pair, belonging to a member of his audience, staring at him.

It was an established practice for the Director of the Staff College to be a member of the Preparatory Promotion Boards, for seaman officers' promotion to commander, and to captain. This was composed of two Rear Admirals and two senior Captains, and their job was to provide "shortlists" for the Admiralty Board, who made the final selections. The actual meetings were straightforward, taking a day, but the task of preparing oneself for them for which one went up to MOD by oneself, was not. One had to read all the reports of all the serious candidates (about two hundred), and form one's own view of their comparative suitability. Much preparation had been done already by the appointers, with each batch separated into "Sheep and Goats", and a suggested list of "probables", but *all* the files were made available and one had to make sure no one had been unfairly excluded. I found this personal preparation mentally demanding – forming an impression of every candidate and then placing them in order. It took me a day's work for each rank. I came back so mentally tired that functions at Greenwich were very difficult afterwards, and I had to be careful to go up for this preparatory work on days with free evenings.

-----oOo-----

The subject of promotion leads naturally to my own future. I was due for promotion or retirement at the end of May 1979. All captains served exactly nine years in the rank, and then either became Rear Admirals, or were placed on the Retired List. To help one plan the future one could ask for a formal assessment of one's promotion prospects during the final three years, and the answer was very broad: 'Unlikely,' 'Likely,' or 'Possible.' I did this, and to my surprise was told 'possible' – in fact it was more precise – 'You have a 50/50 chance, old boy.' I was very surprised that my chances were rated as high as that. I had only been promoted to Captain at the last chance. More important, I was "dry" and thus had had no sea command. All dry captains had been formally warned by letter that their chances of promotion were nil – the Navy, understandably, wanted its seaman officers who became admirals to have experience of sea command.

In early January 1979 I was told I had been placed on a short list of two. Four other members of my batch, who were all "high flyers", had already been selected and their names published. I waited several weeks. Finally the Admiral President, Rear Admiral Tony Cooke, sent for me in early March to say 'I am afraid your name has not caught the selector's eye.' I had very mixed feelings – obviously I would have liked the honour and glory of being on the Flag List, and there was one obvious job I would have fitted straight into had I been selected. But there were considerable advantages in retiring as a Captain, at an age and rank that meant a second career was possible. In early May I left Greenwich and the Navy. It seemed rather appropriate that it should be Greenwich; I had been born whilst my father had been on course there, and I was christened in the Naval Chapel.

Departure. May 1979

EPILOGUE
Retirement

... and that we may return in safety,
to enjoy the blessings of the land
with the fruits of our labours ...

(The Naval Prayer)

'Well Bill, this is a very sad occasion, isn't it?' It was the First Sea Lord speaking, and I was sitting in front of him in his office with the famous green baize table cloth I knew so well from my earlier MOD appointments. It was a month after I had left Greenwich for my "terminal leave" and I was making my farewell call on him; all officers of captain's rank and above did this on retirement. I was determined it should not be the equivalent of a wake. 'Oh I don't know, Sir,' I said brightly, 'I'm looking forward to my second career.' He said some polite things about my career in the Navy and a few other matters were discussed. Was there anything I would like to tell him before I went? (There wasn't). My allotted quarter of an hour of his programme was up. I said goodbye. My active career in the Navy was over. It was late May 1979.

I was fifty-three, and had no intention of putting my feet up. In fact, the next fifteen years were some of the most active of my life. We started by moving "sideways" from the main house of our Hampshire home, into the converted coach house and stables, and found it warmer and more comfortable. We sold the main house and garden, and the adjoining field, but kept the rest of the property. I developed, very profitably, what was left of the old farm buildings, and added an extra storey to our new home. I also converted what had been an old chicken run and ploughed field into a beautiful garden with a ha-ha and long views over green fields, which we later opened for charity for several years. During the 1980s our children all grew up and flew the nest, and Antonia and I settled into a stable and happy home life, despite problems of health. I think it fair to say that I returned in safety to enjoy the blessings of the land.

During this period I also set up as a independent naval consultant, and was engaged for fourteen years by one of the major electronics companies. As it was only part-time this fitted in well with my work on the property at home. It was not only enjoyable but very worthwhile, and I could not have done this had I not had a full naval career with my long exposure to naval communications behind me. This could be considered the fruits of my labours.

Interesting though they might be, my retirement years were not part of my active life in the Navy, and memories of them do not belong in this book.

The final supplication of the Naval Prayer is '*that we may return in safety, with a thankful remembrance of Thy mercies*'. I certainly have such a remembrance.

APPENDIX

THE AUTHOR'S PRINCIPAL APPOINTMENTS AND ACTIVITIES

Dates	Appointment etc	Chapter
1940 – 1943	RN College, Dartmouth	1
1944	HMS *Duke of York*	1
1945	HMS *Orion*	2
1946 – 1947	HMS *Vanguard* and Royal Cruise to South Africa	3
1947 – 1948	HMS *Barrosa*	4
1949 – 1950	Long (C) Course, HMS *Mercury*	6
1950 – 1952	HMS *Saintes* and SCO 3rd Destroyer Squadron	4
1952 – 1953	Dagger (C) Course, RN College Greenwich	6
1953 – 1955	Staff of C-in-C Far Ear Station, Singapore	6
1955 – 1956	HMS *Centaur*	5
1956 – 1958	Instructional Staff, HM Signal School	6
1958 – 1959	Staff of Flag Officer, Aircraft Carriers	5
1960	Exercise Analysis and HMS Dryad	5
1961 – 1963	Commander (X), HMS Mercury	8
1964 – 1966	British Naval Staff, Washington, D C., USA	7
1966 – 1969	Admiralty Surface Weapons Establishment, Portsdown	8
1970 – 1972	Naval Plans Division, MOD London	9
1973 – 1974	Captain of the Dockyard and QHM, Gibraltar	10
1974 -1975	Controller of the Defence Communications Network	11
1975 – 1976	Director of Naval Signals, MOD London	11
1977 – 1979	Director, Royal Naval Staff College, Greenwich	12
1979	Retired from Royal Navy	

GLOSSARY

Barge

A motor boat for the personal use of a senior officer. (C-in-Cs coloured Green; other Flag Officers, Dark Blue; other officers, usually Black).

Dagger Communications Course

Advanced communications course which qualified an officer as a "Dagger C". His entry in The Navy List was marked C†. Usually shortened to "Dagger C Course" or colloquially "Dagger Course".

Electronic Warfare

Exploitation of the enemy's use of radio or electronics. Usually divided into active EW, where jammers or deception devices frustrate or mislead; and passive EW, where enemy transmissions are intercepted and analysed for intelligence etc.

Gunroom

Junior officers Mess in larger warships, for midshipmen and sub-lieutenants. In smaller vessels all officers mess in the Wardroom (qv).

HF High Frequency.

The band of radio frequencies used for long range communication before satellite communications rendered them obsolete. Propagation beyond horizon range was by refraction via the ionosphere, making transmissions of low capacity and unreliable.

Long Communications Course

The year long training course, completion of which qualifed an officer as a Communications Specialist. His name in the Navy List was marked C. Usually shortened to "Long C Course" or colloquially "Long Course".

Manning Ship

A nautical method of greeting or ceremonial with its roots in the days of sail, when ships companies manned the yards and the upper deck, and often cheered. In modern times it is of course limited to the upper deck and superstructure.

NAVCOMS

Abbreviation for "Naval Communications Organisation", the extensive arrangements agreed between the US, British, Canadian and later Australian Navies at top level to plan effective communications between them. For details see Chapters 7 and 11.

SATCOMS   Satellite Communications

Use of satellites for communication. For introduction into navies see Chapter 8.

SAVOLS

Abbreviation for "South Africa Volunteers", a scheme introduced for HMS *Vanguard*'s voyage to South Africa in 1947 whereby ratings due for release from war service volunteered to defer this until the ship's return.

SCO

Staff Communications Officer.

SCOT

Abbreviation for "Satellite Communication Terminal". The name given to the twin headed installation introduced into the Royal Navy in the 1970s. See Chapter 8.

Seaboat

A medium sized boat, usually motorized and open decked, suitable for being launched and recovered at sea from ships.

Signals

A term derived from the use of flags for communication between ships before the days of radio. Its use in the Royal Navy lingered for many years, when it was synonymous with "communications".

Transit Posts

Two tall posts, usually painted white, and positioned on shore so that when viewed in line from seaward they marked a safe passage through shoals, or the beginning and end of a measured distance etc.

Wardroom

The officer's Mess (senior officers in large warships). See Gunroom.

UHF Ultra High Frequency

The band of radio frequencies used for short range military communications. Used for inter-communication between warships out to horizon range, and for aircraft out to about 200 miles. Do not propagate via the ionosphere.

INDEX